BEASLEY'S GUIDE TO LIBRARY RESEARCH

Beasley's Guide to Library Research offers straightforward help in navigating the labyrinth of library research. Suitable for novices and experienced researchers alike, this revised classic is an invaluable tool for locating and using materials from research libraries anywhere in the world.

Written and organized for easy access, the book guides the reader step by step through library rules and methods of operation, the effective use of microfilms and various cataloguing systems, and the location of materials using bibliographies, reference books, and periodical indexes. Also covered are the most modern forms of research, including computer databases, interlibrary loan systems, and online computer searches.

Whether the reader is a student, teacher, writer, librarian, or businessperson, *Beasley's Guide to Library Research* provides the essential information that enables all library users to make the most of their research time.

David Beasley was a reference librarian for 28 years at the New York Research Libraries.

Other Books by David Beasley

The Canadian Don Quixote: The Life and Works of Major John Richardson, Canada's First Novelist (Erin, ON: Porcupine's Quill, 1977)

Through Paphlagonia with a Donkey: A Journey through the Turkish Isfendyars (New York: Davus, 1983)

'Introduction,' *Major Richardson's Short Stories* (Penticton, BC: Theytus, 1986) (editor)

The Suppression of the Automobile (Westport, CT: Greenwood, 1988)

How to Use a Research Library (New York: Oxford University Press, 1988)

That Other God (Simcoe, ON: Davus, 1993) (novel)

The Jenny: A New York Library Detective Novel (Simcoe, ON: Davus, 1994)

Hamilton Romance: A Hamilton–Toronto Nexus (Simcoe, ON: Davus, 1996)

Chocolate for the Poor: A Story of Rape in 1805 (Simcoe, ON: Davus, 1996)

Who Really Invented the Automobile? (Simcoe, ON: Davus, 1997)

The Grand Conspiracy: A New York Library Mystery (Simcoe, ON: Davus, 1997)

Douglas MacAgy and the Foundations of Modern Art Curatorship (Simcoe, ON: Davus, 1998)

Pagan Summer (Simcoe, ON: Davus, 1998)

Understanding Modern Art: The Boundless Spirit of Clay Edgar Spohn (Simcoe, ON: Davus, 1999)

Aspects of Love: Helen, Caravetti, Adam (Simcoe, ON: Davus, 2000)

Beasley's Guide to Library Research

DAVID BEASLEY

UNIVERSITY OF TORONTO PRESS
Toronto Buffalo London

ISBN 0-8020-4782-3 (cloth)
ISBN 0-8020-8328-5 (paper)

Printed on acid-free paper

An earlier form of some of the material in this book appeared in *How to Use a Research Library* (New York: Oxford University Press, 1988).

Canadian Cataloguing in Publication Data

Beasley, David, 1931–
    Beasley's guide to library research

    Rev. ed. of: How to use a research library.
    Includes bibliographical references and index.
    ISBN 0-8020-4782-3 (bound)   ISBN 0-8020-8328-5 (pbk.)

    1. Library research – Handbooks, manuals, etc.   2. Research libraries –
    Handbooks, manuals, etc.   3. Research – Methodology – Handbooks,
    manuals, etc.   I. Title.   II. Title: Guide to library research.   III. Title: How
    to use a research library.

    Z675.R45B42 2000   025.5 ′24   C00-931640-X

University of Toronto Press acknowledges the financial assistance to its publishing program of the Canada Council for the Arts and the Ontario Arts Council.

University of Toronto Press acknowledges the financial support for its publishing activities of the Government of Canada through the Book Publishing Industry Development Program (BPIDP).

In memory of Aloysius and Marie Nicholas

Contents

Preface

This short book is intended for the college student, the casual researcher, and the professional researcher and writer. Those unfamiliar with libraries should read this text from the beginning; more experienced readers can go directly to particular sections outlined in the table of contents.

In this revised edition of *How to Use a Research Library* (Oxford University Press, 1988) I have included material on the use of electronic bibliographic aids to find information and locate articles and books, added information on microform resources, and updated bibliographic references.

Procedures are basically the same for all research libraries; they differ in minor ways such as the form of request slip or kind of catalogue. At the end of the book I note some of the differences I have encountered in major research libraries.

There are many levels of research and many different kinds of facts you will need to know. This work will have served its purpose admirably if it helps you apply the most efficient methods of library research to find the bibliographic tools most useful to your own particular needs.

DRB
Simcoe, Ontario
September 1999

BEASLEY'S GUIDE TO LIBRARY RESEARCH

Quick Reference Guide

HOW TO OBTAIN A BOOK OR PERIODICAL

This section is a brief overview for those who want to locate a publication in the library right away or need a quick review of the essentials. Chapter 1 begins a detailed initiation into the use of research libraries. Specific examples and references throughout this book are to the major research libraries, but the general procedures are similar in all research libraries. The following are some points to keep in mind about using a reference section:

1. Books and periodicals in research libraries can only be consulted. You cannot borrow them.
2. There are several catalogues and many ways of finding publications; some you can find only by asking the librarian (for further details, see p. 43).
3. To make a photocopy from a publication, you must obtain a pass from the librarian to take it from the reading room to the photoservice section.
4. If the library does not have the publication available through the catalogues – whether in book or online form, or in deferred status or microform – the librarian can obtain it for you from another library, or in some cases give you a pass to see it in a library within the metropolitan area (see p. 125).
5. When you have located the publication in the catalogue, do not forget to write down the call number on the request slip.

6. To use the Special Collections for rare or manuscript materials (e.g., Print Collection, Rare Book Room, Manuscripts and Archives), you will have to show proof that you are a researcher and may need to obtain a pass from the Office of Special Collections.

Requesting a Publication

When you enter a research library, ask the librarian at the information desk near the main entrance to guide you to the division where the publications you want are located. If you want a reference work, such as an almanac, directory, or encyclopedia, the librarians at the reference desks can tell you where you can take it off the open shelves in the reading rooms. This saves you from using the library catalogues.

In large research libraries, book stacks are closed to the reader. You must file your request slip for a publication at a specified desk and wait for a library page or assistant to retrieve the publication from the stacks. In university libraries, the book stacks are usually open to readers. You are expected to find the stack level on which the publication is stored and retrieve it for use in the reading rooms. University libraries, unlike public research libraries, allow readers registered with them to borrow publications.

Any issue of a periodical that appeared within the year is on the current periodical shelves, where you can request or access it without a call number. But books and issues of periodicals no longer current are in bound form in the stacks or on microform in the microform reading areas. To request these you must find their call numbers in the library's catalogues or in special bibliographies and indexes that act as catalogues (see p. 54). You can find books on your subject by looking in the catalogues under the correct subject heading. Ask a librarian if you have any trouble locating an appropriate heading.

The call number or classmark identifies the location of the publication in the library. (It is listed at the top right-hand corner of a catalogue card entry and often in boldface on the bottom line of a computer entry.) Write down the author and title on a

Fig. 1

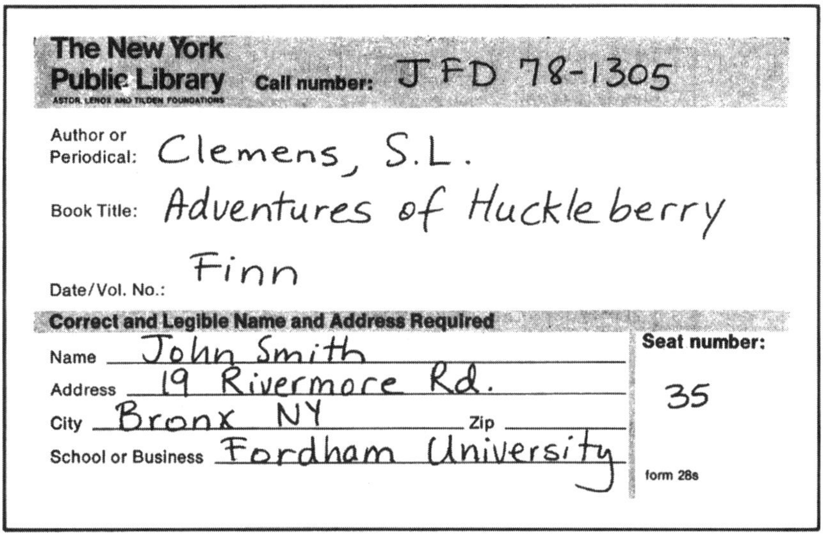

request slip with the call number for a book or microform (see Figure 1). For a serial (e.g., a periodical), include only the periodical's title and the date of the issue with the call number (Figure 2). For an annual report or similar serial, write down the corporate author and title (see p. 59) (Figure 3).

For the past 30 years most research libraries have catalogued new accessions into their computer catalogue and have been gradually converting the entries from their old card and book catalogues into the computer catalogue. You should, therefore, go directly to the computer catalogue to find the call number for the book or periodical you want or to search a subject by standard subject heading or by keyword. If you do not find an older publication there, then look in the book or card catalogues, which are still found in some libraries.

Before computerization, different catalogues spanned different years; you would have had to approach the card catalogue that covered the year in which the publication you wanted was published. For instance, in the New York Research Libraries, if the book you

Fig. 2

The New York Public Library
ASTOR, LENOX AND TILDEN FOUNDATIONS

Call number: JML 77-25

Author or Periodical: Interface; journal of new

Book Title: music research

Date/Vol. No.: Nov. 1982

Correct and Legible Name and Address Required

Name Mary Jackson
Address 31 Main St.
City NY NY   Zip 10007

School or Business

Seat number: 72

form 28s

Fig. 3

The New York Public Library
ASTOR, LENOX AND TILDEN FOUNDATIONS

Call number: SHH

Author or Periodical: Ford Foundation

Book Title: Annual Report

Date/Vol. No.: 1980

Correct and Legible Name and Address Required

Name Mary Jackson
Address 31 Main St.
City NY NY   Zip
School or Business Allardyce Inc

Seat number: 72

form 28s

were looking for was published prior to 1970, you would probably find it listed in the NYPL *Dictionary Catalog of the Research Libraries, 1911–1971* (black volumes; referred to hereafter as NYPL *Dictionary Catalog, 1911–1971*). If it was published after 1970, you would probably find it through the online catalogue computer terminal, which cites publications catalogued since then (see p. 10 for a description of how to use it). Some works are listed only in special division or format catalogues (see p. 77); ask a librarian for help if you do not find a work listed in the main catalogues.

Requesting a Book

1. It is easier to locate a book in most catalogues if you know the author's name. When you know only the title or subject, use a general bibliography like *Cumulative Book Index* or *Books in Print* (see p. 71) to find the author. The computer catalogue uses the standard subject headings set by the U.S. Library of Congress. You must check for the correct subject heading in the bound volumes of the Library of Congress subject headings. You may also use keyword searching in the computer catalogue. If the title is distinctive (e.g., *Encyclopedia of Associations*), you search by title first when online.
2. If you find a publication in a card or book catalogue like the NYPL *Dictionary Catalog, 1911–1971* by subject heading or added entry such as a joint author, write down only the main entry where the request slip requires the author and the title or a condensed version, using the first few words (see Figures 4a,b and 5a,b). Books are located by their main entries within the call numbers. The main entry is often in boldface and is mostly the author entry (see p. 85 for a description of main entry).

   If you request books from the online catalogue and the entry confuses you, often you do not need to use the main entry on the request slip; simply write the call number, which represents a fixed location (Figure 6). If you are ordering a particular volume, do not forget to include the volume number. It is best, however, to write the main entry because some libraries do not have fixed-location call numbers; moreover,

Fig. 4a

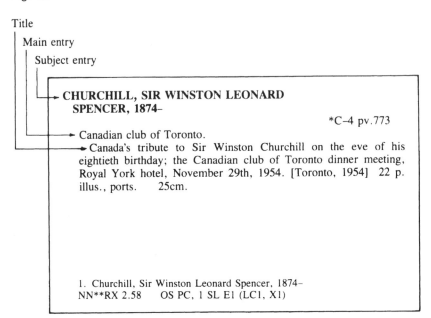

Title

Main entry

Subject entry

CHURCHILL, SIR WINSTON LEONARD SPENCER, 1874–

*C–4 pv.773

Canadian club of Toronto.

Canada's tribute to Sir Winston Churchill on the eve of his eightieth birthday; the Canadian club of Toronto dinner meeting, Royal York hotel, November 29th, 1954. [Toronto, 1954]   22 p. illus., ports.   25cm.

1. Churchill, Sir Winston Leonard Spencer, 1874–
NN**RX 2.58   OS PC, 1 SL E1 (LC1, X1)

Fig. 4b

The New York Public Library
ASTOR, LENOX AND TILDEN FOUNDATIONS

Call number: *C – 4 p.v. 773

Author or Periodical: Canadian Club of Toronto

Book Title: Canada's Tribute

Date/Vol. No.:

Correct and Legible Name and Address Required

Name John Smith

Address 19 Rivermore

City Bronx, NY   Zip

School or Business Fordham University

Seat number: 35

form 28s

Fig. 5a

Title

Main entry

Subject heading

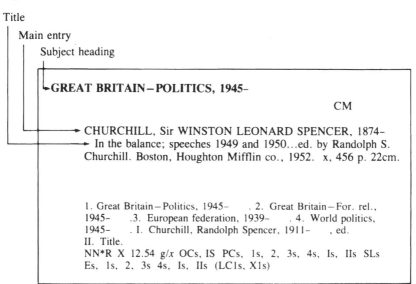

GREAT BRITAIN – POLITICS, 1945–

CM

CHURCHILL, Sir WINSTON LEONARD SPENCER, 1874–
In the balance; speeches 1949 and 1950...ed. by Randolph S.
Churchill. Boston, Houghton Mifflin co., 1952. x, 456 p. 22cm.

1. Great Britain – Politics, 1945–   . 2. Great Britain – For. rel.,
1945–   .3. European federation, 1939–   . 4. World politics,
1945–   . I. Churchill, Randolph Spencer, 1911–   , ed.
II. Title.
NN*R X 12.54 g/x OCs, IS PCs, 1s, 2, 3s, 4s, Is, IIs SLs
Es, 1s, 2, 3s 4s, Is, IIs (LC1s, X1s)

Fig. 5b

Fig. 6 Analysed series title. The dot before the main entry indicates that the book is not catalogued by series. The call number alone will get you the book.

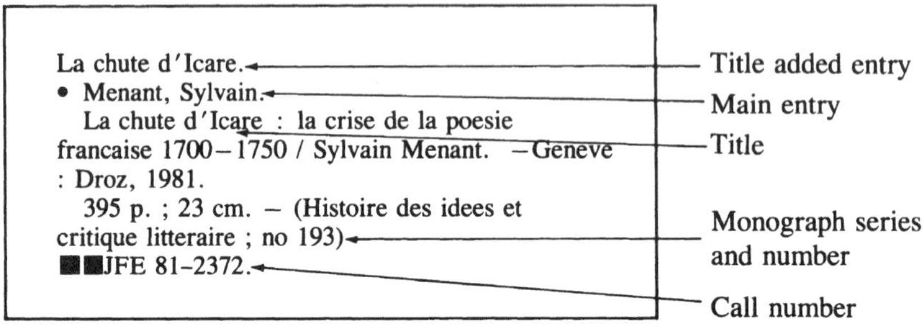
La chute d'Icare.
• Menant, Sylvain.
La chute d'Icare : la crise de la poesie francaise 1700–1750 / Sylvain Menant. –Geneve : Droz, 1981.
395 p. ; 23 cm. – (Histoire des idees et critique litteraire ; no 193)
■■JFE 81-2372.
Title added entry
Main entry
Title
Monograph series and number
Call number

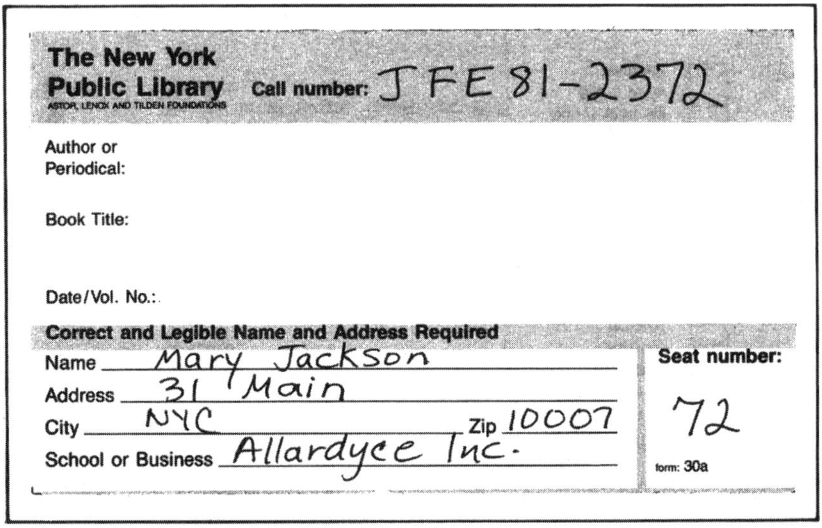
The New York Public Library
ASTOR, LENOX AND TILDEN FOUNDATIONS
Call number: JFE 81-2372
Author or Periodical:
Book Title:
Date/Vol. No.:
Correct and Legible Name and Address Required
Name Mary Jackson
Address 31 Main
City NYC
Zip 10007
School or Business Allardyce Inc.
Seat number:
72
form: 30a

you will need an entry for the book if the call slip is returned to you and you have to check the catalogue for the item again.

The computer or online catalogue includes all the entries (books, pamphlets, periodicals). Instructions on how to use it are kept in pamphlet form nearby. Some systems require you to request the item with the words 'find title,' 'find subject,' or 'find author'; others will show author, title, subject, and key-word choices on the screen. In all cases each successive window on the screen will instruct you how to proceed. Press the return key to bring information to the screen, or, in some cases, click on the search tab.

3. If the book is a volume in a numbered monograph series and has not been analysed in the catalogues (i.e., you cannot find it by author or monograph title), you may find the title of the series in the catalogues. Request the series and the number of the volume you wish to see. You can obtain the series number by looking up the author, subject, or title in the *Cumulative Book Index* (see Figure 7a–f).

Fig. 7a The CBI (Cumulative Book Index) gives you the number of the mono-graphic series by author and title of the pamphlet or book you want to find in the library catalogue. In this case, under author, Price, David Lynn, you find the series 'Washington papers. v 4, no41.'

```
Price. Cecil John Layton
   Gwyn Jones [pub for] the Welsh Arts Council.
      (Writers of Wales) limited ed Q 72p £10 '76
      University of Wales Press
      LC 76-375928
   (ed) See Sheridan. R. B. B. Plays
Price. Christine. 1928-
   Arts of clay. 64p il lib bdg $6.95 '77 Scribner
      ISBN 0-684-15120-0    LC 77-23103
   Arts of wood. 64p il maps lib bdg $6.95 '76 Scrib-
   ner
      ISBN 0-684-14665-7    LC 76-13886
Price. David Lynn
   Oil and Middle East security. (Georgetown Univ.
      Center for Strategic and Int. Studies. Wash-
      ington papers. v4 no41) 84p pa $3 '76 Sage   ◄────
      Publications
      ISBN 0-8038-0791-5    LC 76-54450
```

Fig. 7b You find the series in the library catalogue from the number 1 followed by a dash ('1–').

Main ─────► **The Washington papers.** 1- Beverly Hills [etc.]   ◄─────
entry   Sage Publications [etc.] 1977- 22 cm. CURRENT
                          ISSUES AVAILABLE IN ECONOMICS AND PUBLIC
                          AFFAIRS DIVISION. FULL RECORD OF
                          HOLDINGS IN CENTRAL SERIAL RECORD.
                          Irregular, 1977-79; 8 no. a year, 1980- "Published for the
                          Center for Strategic and International Studies,
                          Georgetown University."   NN 80-4857398
                                        [JLK 80-156] ◄─────── Call
                                                                   number

Fig. 7c

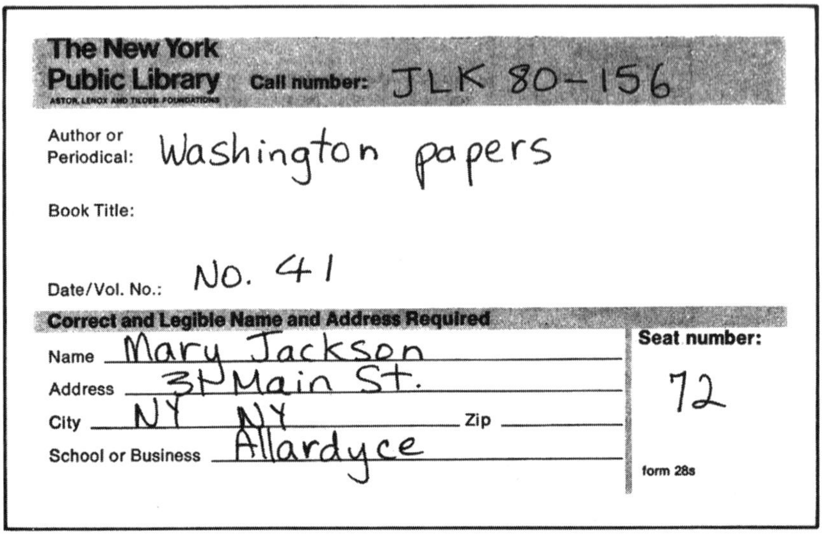
The New York Public Library
ASTOR, LENOX AND TILDEN FOUNDATIONS
Call number: JLK 80-156

Author or Periodical: Washington papers

Book Title:

Date/Vol. No.: No. 41

Correct and Legible Name and Address Required

Name Mary Jackson

Address 3½ Main St.

City NY NY Zip

School or Business Allardyce

Seat number: 72

form 28s

Fig. 7d Sometimes the CBI does not pick up a publication when it should. You cannot find a publication on SALT and security by David Yost in CBI, so you turn to the PAIS *Bulletin* (which covers political subjects) and look it up under the subject heading in the volume covering the year of its publication, 1981. You find that it is in the series 'Washington papers, no. 85' and request it accordingly.

STRATEGIC ARMS LIMITATION TALKS

Cutler, Lloyd N. and Roger C. Molander. Is there life after death for SALT? *Internat Security 6:3-20 Fall '81*

† Gray, Colin S. and Keith B. Payne. SALT: deep force level reductions; final report. Mr '81 v.p. (HI-3195-RR) pa Nonprofit agencies $20; others, price on request —*Hudson inst*

Prepared for the SALT/Arms Control Support Group, U.S. Office of the Assistant to the Secretary of Defense (Atomic Energy).

Feasibility of reductions of strategic force in SALT III.

† Lehman, John F. and Seymour Weiss. Beyond the Salt II failure; foreword by Richard Perle. '81 xxi+195p tables index (Praeger Special Studies/Praeger Sci.) (LC 81-2874) (ISBN 0-03-059448-0) $23.95—*Praeger pub*

Sharp, Jane M. O. Restructuring the SALT dialogue. *Internat Security 6:144-76 Winter '81/'82*

Yost, David S. European security and the SALT process; foreword by Uwe Nerlich. '81 96p bibl (Washington Pa. 85) (Sage Policy Pa.) (LC 81-52788) (ISBN 0-8039-1739-2) pa $4—*Sage pubns* ←——— series

Published for the Center for Strategic and International Studies, Georgetown University.

Quick Reference Guide   13

Fig. 7e You may look in CBI under author or title and find the series that includes the publication, but you cannot find the series in the library catalogue. This is because the library you happen to be using decided to keep this series as an SID (Subject for Individual Decision), which means that the library collects only selected monographs from that series. These monographs may be found in the library catalogue usually by author or title, not by series. Here are two examples of monographic series kept as SIDs.

Heat transfer in nuclear reactor safety; edited by S. George
    Bankoff and N.H. Afgan. (Proceedings of the Inter-
    national Centre for Heat and Mass Transfer. 13) 964p ◄——
    il 1982 Hemisphere
    ISBN 0-89116-223-2   LC 81-13333
       Papers delivered at the Int. Centre for Heat and
    Mass Transfer Seminar on Nuclear Reactor Safety Heat
    Transfer in Dubrovnik. Yugoslavia. Sept. 1-5, 1980
Heat-transfer media
      See also
    Heat pipes
Heat treater's guide; standard practices and procedures for
    steel; edited by Paul M. Unterweiser. Howard E. Boyer,
    James J. Kubbs. Q 493p il 1982 American Soc. for
    Metals
    ISBN 0-87170-141-3   LC 82-8680
Heat treatment of steel See Steel—Heat treatment
Heat treatment, structure, and properties of nonferrous alloys.
    Brooks. C. R. 1982 American Soc. for Metals
Heater, Homer
    A Septuagint translation technique in the Book of Job;
    by Homer Heater. Jr. (Catholic Biblical quarterly.
    Monograph series. 11) 152p pa 1982 Catholic Biblical ◄——
    Assn. of Am.
    ISBN 0-915170-10-8   LC 81-10085

Fig. 7f No. 13 of the Proceedings on the International Centre for Heat and Mass Transfer is found only under the title entry in the library catalogue.

    *Heat transfer in nuclear reactor safety / —
      Hemisphere Pub. Corp., c1982. xii, 964 p. : ill.
      Reg. no.: 0174802
      Call no.: JSE 83-225

Requesting a Periodical Article

1. To find the title and date of the periodical in which an article appears, you look in the periodical indexes that cover the subject of the article. If you know the magazine in which the article appeared, look in *Ulrich's International Periodicals Directory* to see if the magazine is indexed and by which periodical service.

Fig. 8a Note that the 'Bijli, Shah M.' entry is a book. You can tell by form of pagination, that is, '103p.' Look it up in the catalogue by author. In the entry for 'Bird, Graham,' you can tell it is a periodical article because the last line indicates: *Banker* Sept. 1979 (v. 129, p.87).

ECONOMIC ASSISTANCE
See also
Arab states - Economic assistance program
Belgium - Economic assistance program.
Canada - Economic assistance program.
China (People's Republic) - Economic assistance program.
Europe, Western - Economic assistance program.
European economic community - Economic assistance
   program.
Finland - Economic assistance program.
Germany, West - Economic assistance program
International bank for reconstruction and development.
International development association.
Israel - Economic assistance program.
Netherlands - Economic assistance program.
Organization of petroleum exporting countries -
   Economic assistance program.
Technical assistance.
United Nations - Development program
United States - Economic assistance program.

Baqai, Moinuddin. A new framework for international
   financial co-operation for development. *Trade and
   Development p 39-51 Spring '79* this issue $8

Betts, T. F. Development aid from voluntary agencies to
   the least developed countries. *Africa Today 25:49-68
   O/D '78*
      Adapted and updated from a document prepared
   under commission from the United Nations conference
   for trade and development, 1977.

† Bijli, Shah M. Development aid. '79 xii + 103p bibl tables ◄━━━
   index Rs 38—*Shree publishing house, 4056, Ajmeri
   Gate, Delhi-110006, India*
      Overall picture of the concept of aid and the various
   forms assistance has taken.

Bird, Graham. An integrated programme for finance and
   aid: shortcomings in the existing arrangements for
   providing the developing countries with finance and aid
   could be met by establishing a new international
   development organisation funded through the creation
   of SDRs [special drawing rights], thus introducing a
   link between the creation of international liquidity and
   the provision of aid. *Banker (London) 129:87+ S '79* ◄━━━

Fig. 8b

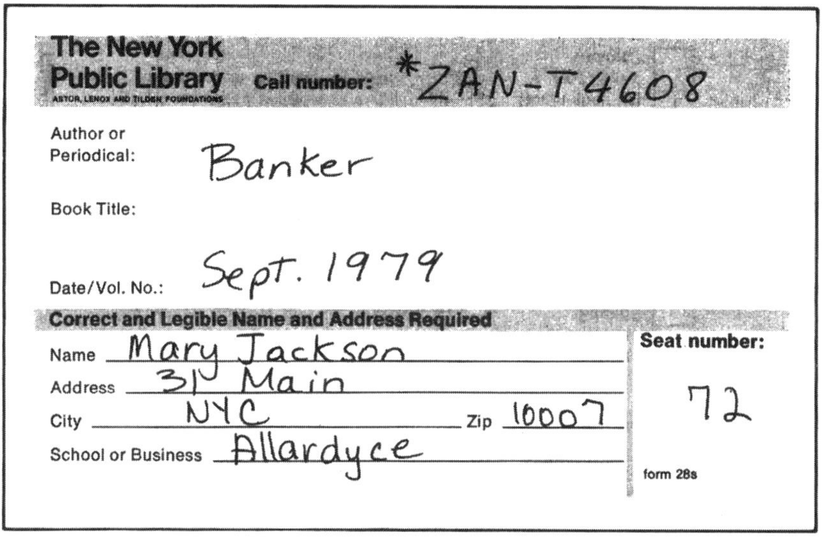
The New York Public Library
ASTOR, LENOX AND TILDEN FOUNDATIONS
Call number: *ZAN-T4608

Author or Periodical: Banker

Book Title:

Date/Vol. No.: Sept. 1979

Correct and Legible Name and Address Required

Name Mary Jackson

Address 31st Main

City NYC Zip 10007

School or Business Allardyce

Seat number: 72

form 28s

2. Most periodical indexes list by subject. Some, such as the *Readers' Guide to Periodical Literature,* index by author as well. Note for yourself the page numbers of the article within the volume (and the author and title of the article, if you will not remember it). Enter on the request slip *only* the title of the periodical and the date of the article (Figure 8a on p. 14 and 8b on p. 15).
3. To find the call number for a periodical, first check whether a handy reference file to periodicals exists from which you can get the call numbers. If you do not find it in the handy file, look in the library catalogues. You should know that libraries catalogue only the first number of a series; they leave an open entry (e.g., v. 1–■), indicating successive volumes added to the first when they are received. Therefore, if you want a 1990 volume of a periodical that began publication in 1920, you would find its call number in the card or book catalogue if it has not been converted to the online catalogue. If the periodical began in 1974 and the library switched to online cataloguing, as many did in 1972, it will be listed in the online

catalogue. If it began publication in the past year or two, it may not yet be entered in the catalogues, but you may find it in the current periodical section.

CD-ROMs as Indexing Services

A great many periodical indexes are available on CD-ROM (compact disc read-only memory). These indexes often cover many years, thus making a search faster and easier than thumbing through the bound volumes for subject entries. You may wish to use the bound volumes if you think that the subject heading or keyword approach on disc is too direct for your kind of search. For instance, sometimes a search requires a broader approach, such as using 'see also' references, in which book indexes are generally more helpful. Some indexes, however, are kept only on CD-ROM. When searching a CD-ROM, follow the directions given on the screen. The indexing on CD-ROMs generally follows the indexing format in book indexes. Since CD-ROMs go back only a certain number of years, you will have to use the bound indexes for magazine and newspaper articles issued decades ago.

Since subscriptions to CD-ROM databases are expensive, you will have to visit your research library to use its online services for free access. The stand-alone CD-ROM station is being replaced by a networking arrangement: the database is loaded locally by a library and made available at other CD-ROM stations in affiliated libraries – say, for example, on a university campus – and access to it over the local Web is restricted to university students, faculty, and personnel. Since printed materials are becoming more costly, research libraries have cooperated by sharing indexes through online networking. In the case of very expensive databases, which some libraries cannot afford, only one of a consortium of libraries buys the printed volumes and lends them on request to other libraries. Many databases, however, can be found on the World Wide Web and offer direct access to consumers by end-user pricing, that is, by creating different versions of the database for different user groups. Most university libraries make all online resources available remotely (off-campus) to their user community.

Check for the periodical in *Ulrich's International Periodical Directory* to see whether its indexing service is on CD-ROM and online. *Ulrich's*, volume 5, gives you sections on Serials Available on CD-ROM and Serials Available Online with URL and vendor.

Using a CD-ROM

You will find instructions on how to use each database beside the CD-ROM monitors in libraries. Many databases are on one monitor. You click on 'Start' and go to 'Select Programs' or click on the appropriate icon, where you choose the database you wish to search, in this case CPI, *Canadian Periodicals Index*. Use the 'F' keys at the top of the keyboard: F1 for help, F2 to browse, F3 to display any item, F10 to exit, and so on. Use the arrow keys to move from one display to another, the backspace to erase letters, and the Esc (escape) key to leave the database. You can ask by keyword or words; for instance, when you type 'research and libraries' and press Enter, you are given 104 hits or citations to articles – too many. Use the Boolean approach of AND, OR, NOT (see under 'Data Banks or Databases' in Chapter 1); you can bracket together synonyms; you can truncate words with the symbol * – for example, strik* for strikes, strikers, striking, strikeouts, and so on. If you type in '(research and libraries) and online' and press Enter you get one hit. Press F3 (display) and the citation comes up as follows:

> Title: Lawyer's guide to the online galaxy: legal research and communications using computers. *Canadian Law Libraries*, vol.17, no.1. February 1992, Page 31–2. Subject: Book reviews; Computers – legal use; Online bibliographic searching.

This is a review of a book in the *Canadian Law Libraries* journal. Search in the library catalogue for the call number to the periodical and request volume 17, or, if in a university library, fetch volume 17 from the stacks.

Filing Request Slips

In the General Research Division

After you have filled out the request slip with call number, author, title (and date or volume number if necessary), and your address, take it to the file clerk at the desk designated for submitting call slips. In some cases the requested item will be brought to your seat number, which you have written on the slip; in other cases you will have to call back in half an hour for the item. In the New York Public Research Libraries, for example, the clerk will give you a card with a number on it and directions to proceed to the light indicators either in the North or the South Reading Hall. When your number lights up on the indicator board, present your card to the clerk behind the counter and you will receive the material you requested, or your slip will be returned with directions explaining why you did not receive the material (see p. 74).

In the Subject Divisions or Special Collections

Before you hand your request slip to a librarian, you must select a seat number from a table in the reading rooms and write this number in the lower right-hand corner of the request slip. A library page will bring the material to you at your seat. (This is the procedure followed in the main reading halls of the British Library and the Bibliothèque Nationale.)

PUBLICATIONS IN MICROFORM

The catalogue entry should indicate whether an item is in microform. If the call number does not indicate it is held by a subject division, you request this material in the microform reading area. There are microform reading rooms also in subject divisions. In the NYP Research Libraries and generally in other libraries, if the material you want has a call number starting with *Z–, it is on microfilm. If the call number begins with *X–, it is on microfiche.

Much of the material on microform is not catalogued. You must use special bibliographic tools to obtain it. Ask a librarian for guidance (see p. 82).

INTERLIBRARY LOAN (ILL)

The Interlibrary Loan Departments (which are sometimes given titles such as Cooperative Services) can obtain a book from another library for you if your library does not have it. (For sources to check, see p. 20.) You can also arrange here for articles from periodicals not in the library to be reproduced in other libraries and forwarded to you. Some of the research libraries no longer have Loan Departments: in the New York Public Research Libraries, for instance, you can locate the publication you want on the online RLIN Bibliographic file called Eureka, which will give you the libraries holding the publication with the call number. You will print out the information and drop it in a specially designated box in whichever division covers the subject of the publication and the librarians of that division will get it for you. (For more on RLIN, see p. 122.) You can also use the WorldCat online terminal for interlibrary loans. It is the union catalogue for the Online Computer Library Center (OCLC), which gives access to more than 37 million records in 370 languages and the resources of over 5,500 libraries, resource centres, and document suppliers. A unique link between OCLC Interlibrary Loan and the OCLC First Search service lets library users inititate requests for publications online, if the library has activated this service. The First Search databases provide electronically produced forms for you to fill out.

The steps you follow are these:

1. Verify the publication on the WorldCat database.
2. Find potential lenders on the WorldCat.
3. Use OCLC ILL Custom Holdings to display the libraries with which your research library has specific lending arrangements.
4. Find your lending library's ILL policies through the OCLC Name-Address Directory. OCLC fills 95 percent of the requests it receives. OCLC sends your electronic request to each potential lender, tracks your request online, confirms the receipt of the item, and updates the ILL transaction record.

Aside from electronic databases and Internet access to library holdings through such search engines as WorldCat and Eureka, some standard book sources are the *National Union Catalog* of pre-1956 imprints and continuations; The *Union List of Serials* and continuations (e.g., *New Series Titles*); Winifred Gregory's *American Newspapers, 1821–1936*; Gregory's *List of the Serial Publications of Foreign Governments, 1815–1931*; *National Register of Microform Masters*; and other titles listed under Microforms on p. 102.

The British Library Online Services, Blaise, taps into 21 databases with more than 18.5 million bibliographic records. It can be accessed by a 'user-friendly graphical interface' on the World Wide Web. A direct online link to the British Library Document Supply Centre lets you request items for loan. You may order photocopies of items over the library's Web page.

RESEARCH ON THE INTERNET

You can find research libraries that have materials you are looking for by calling up their catalogues on the World Wide Web from your home computer. For example, here are Web addresses for home pages of some important libraries with free access (some university libraries restrict online access to their catalogues):

The New York Public Library: http://www.nypl.org
The Library of Congress: http://www.loc.gov (Locus, the

Library of Congress Online System, has over 30 million records that are accessible to the public).

The British Library: http://portico.bl.uk

La Bibliotheque Nationale de France: http://www.bnf.fr

Harvard University Libraries: http://hollisweb.harvard.edu

U.S. National Library of Medicine: http://www.nlm.nih.gov

University of California at Berkeley: http://library.berkeley.edu (This provides access to its various catalogues, finding guides, electronic indexes, and abstracts, etc.).

University of Toronto (Canada) Libraries: http://www.library. utoronto.ca

COPAC: http://www.copac.ac.uk/copac (This provides online access to the catalogues of the largest research libraries in Ireland and the United Kingdom, including Oxford's Bodleian Library, Cambridge University, Edinburgh University, Glasgow University, Trinity College Dublin, etc.)

OCLC (Online Computer Library Center): http://www.oclc. org (This gives access to more than 24,000 libraries in 63 countries).

OCLC Europe: http://www.oclc.org/oclc/europe (This gives access to more than 900 libraries in 37 countries. It lists OCLC member libraries with home pages on the Web, gives information about the libraries, and makes their catalogues accessible.)

Gabriel is the World Wide Web server for Europe's national libraries and provides a single point of access for the retrieval of information about their services, functions, and collections.

You may not find older publications through the Internet because they have not been converted to the library's online catalogue. You will have to visit a research library to look in its book catalogues or in national or special bibliographies for a citation to the publication you want. You may find articles in current publications on the Internet and print them out. This is also true of government and nongovernment documents.

The Internet has been called 'a library without a catalogue.'

Books such as Timothy Malloy's *The Writers' Internet Handbook* (New York: Allworth Communications, 1997) and Peter Morvill's *The Internet Searchers Handbook* (New York: Neal-Shulman, 1996) attempt to help you find what you are looking for on the Internet.

Most Internet searching is done by means of search engines such as Yahoo, by keyword, although some methods, like the Boolean approach, are more useful. Many Internet sites can give you facts quickly. For example:

- If you want the latest currency rates, call up the Universal Currency Converter Online (http://www.xe.net/currency). The Interactive Currency Table has a form that reads 'Show me a currency table in units of ____.' Choose a currency, and it will compare it with all other currencies.
- Name Base (http://www.pir.prg) contains names of individuals, corporations, and groups. It is a searchable name index of people in the news related to the military, organized crime, intelligence agencies, scandals, terrorism, UFOs, and other topics.
- For free access to biographical information on notable figures, past and present, with dates of birth and death, professional awards, literary and artistic works, and so on, you can search by name, keyword, or expression the Notable Citizens of Planet Earth Biographical Dictionary (http://www.s9.com/biography).
- The Web of Culture site lists capital cities, currencies, holidays, languages, resources, religions, and so on (http://www.webofculture.com).
- The U.S. Travel Warnings site (htttp://www.go-Global.com) gives you up-to-date advisories on travel security, crime problems, and visa requirements in the nations of the world; or you can simply search a database such as Alta Vista with the keywords 'travel-warnings' for travel advice issued by many nations on the Internet.
- For searching the Internet, some databases have Starting Points. For example, the Academic and Distributed Computing Services (http://www.micro.umn.edu) provides access to pop-

ular Internet resources such as Yahoo, which categorizes by subject area, or WebCrawler or Switchboard for searching for information on a topic. The Argus Clearinghouse (http://www.clearinghouse.net) gives annotated guides to Internet sites related to practically every subject.

- An example of a Web site as a grab bag of information is the Useless Information Site: http://home.nycap.rr.com/useless.
- Finally, a growing number of sites offer free full texts such as the On-Line Books Page (http://www.cs.cmy.edu/books.html), where you may choose from over 9,000 books and 25,000 songs, including banned books and foreign-language books, and links to other book sites. The National Digital Library offers the U.S. Library of Congress's American history collection dating from the sixteenth century and includes George Washington's diaries and Walt Whitman's notebooks (memory.loc.gov/ammem/mdquery.html). The English Server (eserver.org/) gives 20,000 texts in the humanities including essays, fiction, journals, theory, drama, and poetry. You may read the Greek and Roman classics in translation at http:classics.mit.edu/Browse/authors.html and at http://www. perseus.tufts.edu. There are sites for the works of individual poets and authors as well. A useful site is the Scout Report, a weekly publication offering a selection of new and newly discovered Internet resources of interest to researchers and educators: http://scout.cs.wisc.edu/report/sr/current/index.html.

Whether or not you have conducted Internet research before visiting a library, you must be clear about what you want when you enter.

LIBRARIANS AND HOW TO DEAL WITH THEM

'When I go into a bank, I get rattled,' a Stephen Leacock story begins. 'The clerks rattle me ...' The same can often be said about research libraries and librarians.

So the first thing you must learn is to overcome any hesitancy in approaching librarians; they are trained to direct you to the correct sources for using the collections. Research librarians hold not only advanced degrees in library science but often advanced degrees in another field, making them subject specialists in that field as well. As you become familiar with the library and its staff, you will get to know which librarians have the special skills you need to help you in your particular areas of interest. Be explicit in describing your information needs to the librarians. Because librarians are often hard-pressed for time, you should formulate your questions carefully before you ask them. Your ability to clearly describe your research needs enables librarians to give you the full benefit of their knowledge and training. If you follow the advice contained in this book, your greater library knowledge will increase the librarians' cooperation and respect for you as a serious researcher.

The procedures for finding materials in large research libraries are more involved than those for smaller libraries. But the first thing to remember is that the research is your responsibility. Research librarians are not there to do your work for you, but to direct you to the reference sources where you will find the facts required for your specific subject areas of research. However, this should not prevent you from asking questions in pursuit of your research, for most of what you need can be found in any modern research library.

RULES AND HOW TO DEAL WITH THEM

For the most part, researchers do not know the rules of library procedure until they break one. The rules exist for the practical purpose of protecting the collection as well as controlling the location and retrieval of the books, periodicals, manuscripts, and other works in the extensive stack areas and reading rooms of a large reference library. At most research libraries you cannot carry books from one division to another, or from outside the library into the main reading room, without a special pass. At some libraries, readers need passes to enter special divisions or to use pens, typewriters, and recording equipment.

Some rules can be bent. If you find your ability to pursue your research is obstructed by a particular library rule, explain your needs to the librarian and ask if an exception can be made in your case. The librarian will try to accommodate you if at all possible. One rule, however, remains steadfast: the prohibition against borrowing or removing books from most research libraries. But you can usually photocopy materials essential to your work.

Chapter 1

General Approach to the Research Library

Elementary, my dear Watson

WHAT A RESEARCH LIBRARY OFFERS

A research library is an extensive storehouse of information classified for quick retrieval. Several large research libraries have holdings covering all subjects – for example, the New York Public Library, the Library of Congress, the British Library, and the Bibliothèque Nationale. It is these libraries that concern us in this book. Hundreds of smaller research libraries collect only in certain subject or language areas. These have to be used almost exclusively when research is done on specific subjects such as theology, medicine, and law. Other important research libraries are university libraries, which shape their collections to the needs of their students and faculty.

What does a research library do for you that a branch library cannot do?

A research library does three things:

1. It provides depth of information: it keeps many books on a subject, including all scholarly works, whereas most branch libraries have room for only a few select books that are popular.

2. It provides a historical view: a research library keeps one copy of most works as a permanent record, so that you can find almost everything published on a given subject, whereas a branch library discards older books to make room for the latest books on a subject.
3. It aims at comprehensiveness: a research library collects widely all forms of publications, whereas the branch library is restricted to collecting materials that can circulate and selecting only a small reference and periodical section to meet the needs of the local community it serves.

WHERE TO BEGIN

Can you get information from a research library without visiting the library?

Most research libraries provide a telephone information service that answers those questions a librarian can research within minutes. Moreover, the use of information-retrieval systems in the home or office is becoming widespread. The Internet will lead you to several databases, from which you can retrieve brief, factual replies to your questions. Most large research and university libraries are online, and researchers can call up their computer catalogues to determine if they have particular publications. For research demanding more than simple facts, bibliographic references, and articles available online, however, you must visit the library.

What do you do first when you enter a research library?

Most research libraries require a reader's pass, which you can acquire (sometimes for a fee) at the administrative office. In the Bibliothèque Nationale of Paris, for example, you must provide a passport-size photograph of yourself. At the New York Public Library (except for Special Collections) and the Library of Congress in Washington, DC, however, readers' passes are not required. If you are not connected to the university library as a student or alumnus, you should ask for permission to use the library and explain the subject of your research.

Some research libraries, such as NYPL, have separate subject or form departments: art, economics, genealogy, microforms, science, and others. You go to the central information desk to get directions to the department that covers your subject. Other libraries – the British Library in London, for example – have one main reading room with separate departments only for keeping materials such as government publications, manuscripts, and rare books.

**On entering the reading rooms what sort of responses
to your questions can you expect from the reference librarian?**

The librarian may have to ask you for more details, or may rephrase your question to get a better understanding of what you are seeking. Then you can be directed to a specific section in a specific area, as follows:

Reference Shelf Area

1. To find a list of books on a particular subject, a bibliography is recommended.
2. For a biographic sketch, appropriate biographical dictionaries or the *Biography Index* are suggested.
3. For the address of a company, a directory of corporations is useful.
4. The latest population census can be found on the open shelves.
5. To find out how much water flows over Niagara Falls, a ready-reference almanac can be used.
6. To find a periodical article on a certain subject, the correct periodical indexes are the source.

Some research libraries, such as NYPL, indicate reference shelf books with '*R–' or 'R–' before the call number. Others use '(REF)' under the first letters of the call number, which indicate a specific subject area on the open shelves.

Catalogue Area

1. To find a book by a certain author, you can use the library catalogues (see the Quick Reference Guide for a quick summary of procedures for finding classmarks or call numbers and filling out request slips).
2. For more biographical information about a person than is provided by the biographical directories on the reference-room shelves, the librarian may suggest checking the library catalogues under the person's name as subject.
3. If you cannot find books in the catalogues under a certain subject, perhaps the cataloguers used a different subject heading, in which case the librarian can suggest other headings from the subject heading guide.
4. If you want back issues of a periodical or an annual corporation manual, the librarian can help you find the classmark by directing you to the catalogues that list the series.

Data Bank Area

These areas in libraries have grown so much in recent years that it is common to find over 120 periodical databases online in a subject division.

1. To find complete bibliographic information on a specific subject quickly, you or the librarian can hook into the appropriate CD-ROM or computer data bank such as ERIC and EUSIDIC and obtain the bibliographic printout generally for free (the library may have to charge you a fee for some data banks and/ or for printing).
2. To quickly obtain facts on a news event within the past ten years or so, you can research a newspaper's data banks in storage retrieval for free, if the library subscribes. Libraries provide Internet service free, and often provide e-mail service for readers.

Special Collections Area

To find a rare book, an author's manuscript, the correspondence of a politician, or an Audubon print, the librarian will direct you to the special collections office for a pass to visit the particular collection you need.

What are the reference works and how do you find them?

Reference works are dictionaries, directories, encyclopedias, almanacs, biographical works, standard editions, bibliographies, periodical indexes, and other aids for finding information in the collection. They are self-contained – that is, they have their own indexes – and give basic information without requiring you to search further.

Reference works are available for use on the open shelves of the reading rooms, whereas the bulk of the research collection is on closed shelves, from which (in most research libraries) the books can be retrieved only by library personnel.

ONLINE SEARCHING

Online searching is a teleprocessing system in which data are transmitted immediately from a computer to remote terminals, or vice versa, by means of communications facilities such as common telephone lines. When you are online to the computer, you send a question and receive an answer to that question in a few seconds.

In this cybernetic age, library readers gravitate to the computer monitors when they enter a library division, and for good reason, because the information they need is sometimes best found in a computer database rather than a book or periodical. For certain expensive online host carriers on the Internet, the librarian interviews you to determine whether online searching should be used, which database should be contacted, and how much money you wish to spend in the search. Searches on these databases are limited to half an hour or so, not only to save the library from paying high research fees but because other patrons may be waiting to use the computer. Research libraries have special librarians who do searching for businesses and organizations for a fee. For other databases, you will be able to research them directly from Internet terminals provided by the library at no cost.

In the United States there are three major network lines: Telenet, Tymnet, and Uninet. Their host services, such as DIALOG, and the data banks these services provide in North America and abroad (through Euronet), are complicated and diverse.

The Terminal

The terminal has a screen and an attached printer that enables you to produce a record of the search. Thousands of terminals can call on the computer at the same time. The magnetic disks store the information. You type your request, and the computer displays the answer. International telecommunications networks carry the message, and modems (*mo*dulator *dem*odulators) convert the digital messages, which the terminal and the computer understand, to analog messages that can be transmitted over telephone lines.

Networks

Tymnet, Telenet, and Uninet are largely North American telecommunications networks that have hundreds of nodes into which you can dial access to almost all the major American online services. They have nodes in Europe (Brussels, Frankfurt, Geneva, The Hague, London, Paris, Vienna, Rome) and other parts of the world (Hong Kong, Manila, San Juan, Singapore). For example, in Great Britain the post office has set up the International Packet Switching Service, which allows British searchers to access computers in North America and North American searchers to access computers in Britain. (A network node is a minicomputer that does preliminary checks and organizes the sending of messages between searcher and computer.)

Euronet provides access to scientific and technical information for all member countries of the European Community. It links a wide range of existing European information retrieval services, such as the European Space Agency's Information Retrieval, Blaise, Infoline, DIMDI (the West German medical information service), ARIANE (a French service in civil engineering), and ITF (an international textile information service based in Paris); it also links to other networks such as Scannet (operated by Nordfosk, the Scandinavian Council for Applied Research) and can be accessed from North America.

Information Retrieval Services

Information retrieval services are vendors of the information carried over the telecommunications networks. They control online access to this information, which is held in data banks. Among them are DIALOG, owned by the Lockheed Missiles and Space Company, with over 600 databases and millions of records; Bibliographic Retrieval Services, Inc. (BRS), which allows full-text searching and access to databases such as Medlars, ERIC, NTIS; Systems Development Corporation (SDC); and EUSIDIC, which emphasizes data banks originating in Europe.

Data Banks or Databases

Data banks, or databases, are electronic index sources usually also available in printed book form, which we shall discuss as periodical indexes and abstracts. For instance, the printed PAIS *Bulletin* is available on CD-ROM and in the data bank reached through DIALOG information retrieval services; the nonprinted *Executive Information Service* is reached through BRS. Many new databases have been developed for online access only.

An essential reference work is the two-volume *Gale Directory of Databases.* It gives you worldwide coverage of over 11,500 databases in all subject areas that are available for rapid retrieval by a computer. Databases at first provided only bibliographic citations, like periodical indexes, but now they often provide the full text of articles. Access to these online articles over the Web is by subscription, but some bibliographic databases are linking to these online versions.

The following are brief descriptions of some databases, including the information they provide:

- *Lexis* gives instant access to the opinions in law cases (including

the judge's words) and to cases that have been overruled. It
includes U.S. Supreme Court cases from 1905, Courts of
Appeals cases from 1940, District Courts cases from 1960,
National Labor Relations Board cases from 1972, and the Commerce Clearing House Labor Cases series.

- *Nexis* gives instant access to the full text of newspapers, magazines, newsletters, and wire services. Newspapers are available
the day after they are published, weekly magazines one week
after publication, monthly magazines three weeks after publication, and wire services 12 to 48 hours after they are carried over
the wire.

  Law libraries can afford these online services, but research
  libraries in general must seek smaller versions that are pack-
  aged by companies for the needs of particular users. The
  LEXIS-NEXUS Academic Universe targets the academic library
  market, offering a subset of the content of these databases, and
  markets them through the Congressional Information Service
  (http://www.cispubs.com/acaduniv/), which offers consortia
  pricing to large groups of academic libraries and carries adver-
  tising to help subsidize the cost.

- *Bureau of National Affairs* (BNA) provides data bank information on labour contract settlements, basic patterns in the settlements of contracts, work stoppages, National Labor Relations
Board election reports, labour arbitration cases, and access, by
chemical name, to U.S. government regulations in the Code of
Federal Regulations and in the computer tapes of chemical
abstracting companies.

- The United States Government Printing Office gives free Internet access to most government publications such as the *Monthly
Catalog,* the *Federal Register,* Congressional Hearings, Bills, *GAO
Reports, Public Laws, Export Administration Regulations* and the
titles mentioned in the section on Government Publications
(see p. 107) (http://www.access.gpo.gov).

- CBCA (Canadian Business and Current Affairs) provides
online access to full-text articles appearing in over 200 Canadian periodicals, 300 popular magazines, and 10 newspapers
since 1995 by author, title, and subject keyword. These services

and many like them are available on the Internet by subscription, but research libraries provide free access to the public.

All computer retrieval services are somewhat alike, although they differ in that they require their own peculiar computer language. Microcomputers are able to translate computer languages between computer services and thus make available all the data banks in all the information retrieval services around the globe.

Before you connect with the retrieval system, you can prepare for your search offline on your microcomputer to save on the cost of the online search. You can also store information, such as scientific abstracts from a large international database, locally on a microcomputer system, which saves the cost of repeatedly calling up the database on the time-sharing telecommunications network. This process is called *downloading*.

To make your search, follow these steps:

1. Connect the computer and log on to the online system.
2. Select the file (database) to be searched.
3. Enter and combine search terms.
4. Print the results.
5. Log off and disconnect. (The cost of the search will appear on the screen when you log off.)

You should decide on the descriptors you intend to use in your request before you connect to the computer – that is, author's name, title, subjects, or concepts should be clear to you before you begin.

If, when online such as in the DIALOG database, you find that a subject descriptor does not appear to be finding the number of articles you expected, you may type 'e' for expand, followed by a descriptor (e.g., 'e economic'). A number indicating how frequently it is used as a descriptor appears: 'e economic 5.' The computer then displays terms – 'economical 25, economics 510, economist 320' – and you can decide which terms to use for the best results.

The command language or terminology you use is specific to

the information retrieval service you call on; libraries may keep the manuals beside the terminals for ready reference.

When you are put through to the system, you are given the date, the time, and some system news. The system gives you a prompt, indicating that the computer is ready to receive information. You type in the file you want (determined ahead of time by consulting the list of databases).

Because of the vast amount of information that is instantly available if you know how to tap it, you must be precise in your questioning; otherwise, you will be flooded with information you do not want. You look for keywords appropriate to your subject, and develop connectors with Boolean logic, which is a technique for performing computer searches by combining or excluding words, numbers, or characters. For example, AND, OR, and NOT are connectors between subject terms or 'concepts,' as they are called. AND means mutually exclusive; CHEESE AND BREAD requests retrieval of all citations to publications dealing with cheese and bread together, not to publications dealing with cheese only or bread only. If you want the latter, you type CHEESE OR BREAD. You introduce NOT into your command when you want to eliminate a concept: Thus CHEESE NOT BREAD ensures that you will not get citations to publications dealing with the making of cheese sandwiches, for example, but you will get citations to publications on the production and marketing of cheese.

Suppose you approach a retrieval service such as DIALOG. You want to link into DIALOG's database(s) that will best answer your question (e.g., What wars have been fought in the Near East in recent years?). You choose the two or three concepts that best represent your question (e.g., Near East and war). You survey the thumbnail descriptions of the databases to determine the ones you will use, then call up database DIALINDEX (file 411), which searches all the other databases in DIALOG. You type the first of the designated file numbers of the databases you have selected (e.g., File 49, PAIS International) and your concepts, Near East and war. The same is done with each file, in turn (e.g., File 111 [National Newspaper Index], File 132 [Standard and Poor's News]).

The computer tells you how many items of each of your concepts are in each separate database. From this, you select the database(s) with the highest number of 'hits' and plug directly into it or them in turn. Type in your concepts 's Near East and war' for 'select Near East and war,' and carry on the search, expanding or refining it as you go along (see Figure 1.1).

When you have brought your search to the final number of citations, you call up the citations on the screen. You may print them out right away, or, if there are several, ask DIALOG to print them and send them to you for less cost.

You can access DIALOG databases from your home computer over the Internet (http://www.dialogweb.com/). DIALOG Web has a number of innovative features such a new Database Directory that lets you browse DIALOG databases by subject and integrated Web Bluesheets that provide database content, capabilities, and the most current rate information. DIALOG issues a *Pocket Guide* giving a brief summary of the DIALOG commands and features that you are likely to use most often.

Strategy

For precision in searching, you need to choose a strategy. First, decide whether to employ the controlled vocabulary, like 'Poetry, Romantic – Great Britain,' which is unique to each database, or to use free-text terms, like 'romantic (w) poets and English (w) poets' ('w' means 'with' and must be used to link words in the same concept), which are used by DIALOG to enclose phrases in one concept. Other databases use parentheses and quotation marks like '(courtly love) and (French poetry)' or ' 'hill tribes' and Thailand.' Controlled vocabulary searches tend to be more formally precise because they pick up items by the subject headings given by the indexers, whereas free-text searches bring a higher recall because, when the whole text of the abstract is searched, the term is more likely to be encountered.

Second, adopt one of three basic strategies:

1. the *building block* strategy, in which you develop concepts sepa-

Fig. 1.1 Sample search

```
*U001  000 CONNECTED TO 41500026


ENTER YOUR DIALOG PASSWORD
xxxxxxxxL LOGON FILE1 FRI 22JUN84
11:48:29 PORTO32

** SORTS ARE NOT WORKING IN 1,10 & 506**
**FILES 139,140,328,648 ARE NOT WORKING*
** FILE 221 IS NOT AVAILABLE ON TYMNET
** OR TELENET                          **
DIALOG NEWS (ENTER ?NEWS FOR DETAILS):
  NEW THIS MONTH:
    ONTAP EMBASE (FILE 272)
  FREE TIME IN JUNE:
    EI ENGINEERING MEETINGS (FILE 165)
      --$49.50 COMBINED CONNECT TIME
      AND TYPES/DISPLAYS
  ANNOUNCEMENTS:
    UNINET AND DIALNET (VIA LONDON)
    MOVED TO DIALOG SYSTEM C
    PRICE CHANGE ON COFFEELINE (FILE
    164) NOW IN EFFECT.
? B 411                                          (Begin file 411, Dialindex)
         22JUN84 11:48:52 USER29432
    $0.20  0.008 HRS FILE1*
    $0.05  UNINET
    $0.25  ESTIMATED TOTAL COST


FILE411:DIALINDEX(TM)
(COPR. DIALOG INF.SER.INC.)
? SF 49 AND SF 111 AND SF 132                    (I asked for the 3 files at once)

UNKNOWN FIELDS:49 AND SF 111 AND SF 132          (But it can handle only one at a
                                                                           time)
NO FILES SELECTED
? S FILES 49                                     (Okay, select File 49, PAIS)

FILE49:PAIS INTERNATIONAL - 76-84/JUN            (Data base is from 1976 through
                                                  the present date in June 1984)
         FILE ITEMS DESCRIPTION
         ---- ----- -----------
? S NEAR EAST AND WAR
      (49)
              758 NEAR EAST
              1749 WAR
              28  NEAR EAST AND WAR              (28 hits)
? S FILES 111

FILE111:NATIONAL NEWSPAPER INDEX -
79-84/JUN

         FILE ITEMS DESCRIPTION
         ---- ----- -----------
? S NEAR EAST AND WAR
      (111)
              4740 NEAR EAST
              8244 WAR
              823  NEAR EAST AND WAR             (823 hits)
? S FILES 132

FILE132:STANDARD & POORS DAILY NEWS, 79-84       (S&P is an unlikely source,
                                                  but check to see if the
         FILE ITEMS DESCRIPTION                   subject is recorded to have
         ---- ----- -----------                   affected the financial market)
? S NEAR EAST AND WAR
      (132)
              0 NEAR EAST
              38 WAR
              0  NEAR EAST AND WAR               (Sure enough: no items)
```

Fig. 1.1 (cont.)

```
? S NEAR EAST OR WAR
       (132)
                        0 NEAR EAST
                       38 WAR
                       38  NEAR EAST OR WAR          (A little experimental fun)
? B 111                                              (Begin file 111)
           22JUN84 11:56:09 USER29432
    $4.3]  0.123 HRS FILE411 6 DESCRIPTORS
    $0.74  UNINET
    $5.05  ESTIMATED TOTAL COST


FILE111:NATIONAL NEWSPAPER INDEX -
79-84/JUN
(COPR. IAC)
          SET ITEMS DESCRIPTION
          --- ----- -----------
? S NEAR EAST AND WAR

                     4740 NEAR EAST
                     8244 WAR
              1       823  NEAR EAST AND WAR          (Type set 1/brief citation (3)/
? T 1/3/1-3                                           first 3 as a sample)
1/3/1
0849769   DATABASE: NNI FILE 111
  AS GULF WAR WORSENS,  TURKEY MAKES BID
TO ACT AS PEACEMAKER BETWEEN IRAN,
IRAQ.  (INTERNATIONAL NEWS)
  DEMIRSAR, METIN; BOWERS, BRENT
  WALL STREET JOURNAL    SECTION 2   P30(W)
P34(E0 MAY 29 1984
  CODEN: WSJOAF
  COL 1   014 COL IN.                                (The latest entered is the
  ILLUSTRATION; PORTRAIT                             first out)
  EDITION: TUE

1/3/2
0845150   DATABASE: NNI FILE 111
  SAUDI AIRCRAFT COULD ENTER IRAN-IRAQ
FIGHT.
  OBERDORFER, DON
  WASHINGTON POST    V107  PA1  MAY 20
1984
  COL 1   034 COL IN.
  ILLUSTRATION; PHOTOGRAPH
  EDITION: SUN

1/3/3
0843198   DATABASE: NNI FILE 111
  WAR'S UNCERTAIN EFFECT ON OIL; SUPPLIES
SEEN AS ADEQUATE. (PERSIAN GULF)
  DIAMOND, STUART
  NEW YORK TIMES    V133 P25(N) PD1(L)
May 30 1984
  CODEN: NYTIA
  COL 3   025 COL IN.
  ILLUSTRATION; MAP; TABLE; GRAPH
  EDITION: WED
                                              (823 items is too many. Limit
? S PY=1979 AND S1                            them to the first year of the
            159509 PY=1979                    data base, 1979) (51 is still
              2    51  PY=1979 AND S1         too many; I'll come back when
? B 49                                        I think of an additional
           22JUN84 12:00:24 USER29432         descriptor to limit the search.
    $6.05  0.072 HRS FILE111 3 DISCRIPTORS    Meanwhile, begin file 49)
    $0.43  UNINET
    $0.30  3 TYPES
    $6.78  ESTIMATED TOTAL COST
```

Fig. 1.1 (cont.)

```
FILE49:PAIS INTERNATIONAL - 76-84/JUN
(COPR. PAIS INC.)
        SET ITEMS DESCRIPTION
        --- ----- -----------
? S NEAR EAST AND WAR AND S YR=1976
              758 NEAR EAST
              1749 WAR
            0 S YR=1976
        1    0  NEAR EAST AND WAR AND
S YR=1976
? S NEAR EAST AND WAR
              758 NEAR EAST
              1749 WAR
        2    28  NEAR EAST AND WAR
? T 2/3/1-3
2/3/1
   329123    841501124
   THE MIDDLE EAST:
   WAR  DANGERS  AND  RECEDING  PEACE
PROSPECTS  (EMPHASIS ON UNITED STATES
POLICY TOWARD THE REGION).
   FABIAN, LARRY L.
   FOR AFFAIRS ,    62:632-58 NO 3('84),
THIS ISSUE $6.75,
2/3/2
   328220    841306815
   WAR AND "ANTI-PEACE": MIDDLE EAST;
   THE WASHINGTON-TEL AVIV ALLIANCE.
   MEDVEDKO, LEONID.
   NEW TIMES (MOSCOW) ,   P 8-11 NO 2
JA '84,    IL

2/3/3
   308789    831004584
   MORE MUSCLE:   ROLE OF U.S. IN MIDEAST
STRENGTHENS IN WAKE OF THE WAR IN LEBANON;
   ISRAEL'S CRUSHING OF THE PLO (PALESTINE
LIBERATION ORGANIZATION) WEAKENS RADICAL
ARABS AND THEIR SOVIET FRIENDS.

   SEIB, GERALD F.
   WALL ST J ,    200:1+ N 5 '82,
? T 2/5/3
2/5/3
   308789    831004584
   MORE MUSCLE:   ROLE OF U.S. IN MIDEAST
STRENGTHENS IN WAKE OF THE WAR IN LEBANON;
   ISRALEL'S CRUSHING OF THE PLO (PALESTINE
LIBERATION ORGANIZATION) WEAKENS RADICAL
ARABS AND THEIR SOVIET FRIENDS.

   SEIB, GERALD F.
   WALL ST J ,    200:1+ N 5 '82,
   LANGUAGES: ENGL
   DOC TYPE: P
   DESCRIPTORS: *UNITED STATES-- FOREIGN
RELATIONS-- NEAR EAST; *NEAR EAST-- FOREIGN
RELATIONS-- UNITED STATES; *LEBANON--
ISRAELI INVASION, 1982
? LOGOFF
            22JUN84 12:04:18 USER29432
   $4.55   0.066 HRS FILE49 4 DESCRIPTORS
   $0.40   UNINET
   $0.80   4 TYPES
   $5.75   ESTIMATED TOTAL COST
LOGOFF 12:04:19

*U012 000 DISCONNECTED AT REQUEST OF HOST
```

(None of the citations was in 1976!)

(Only 28 in 7½ years)
(Type set 2/brief citation (3)/ the first 3 items)

I have been using free text terms. I would like to see what the controlled vocabulary or subject headings used by PAIS would look like; therefore, I ask the computer to type set 2/full citation (5)/ for the third item only.

(I am logging-off to plan my search better. Already the cost is higher than I expected)

(The host has been DIALOG; the network has been Uninet)

rately and then combine them with Boolean logic, as we illustrated by the 'Near East and war' search example;

2. the *successive fractions* search, in which you begin with a large set on what may be a somewhat vague subject and successively intersect additional concepts to narrow the search to the desired size and specificity; and

3. the *citation pearl growing* search, in which you select a citation known to the database, examine its index terms, recycle them into the search to retrieve additional citations, and repeat the process until you have formulated a strategy.

Once you have a number of bibliographic citations, you can look up their call numbers in the library's catalogues.

WHEN NOT TO USE ONLINE RETRIEVAL

There are a number of questions you should ask yourself before you use online retrieval:

1. Are there databases that cover the subject? For example, the best index source for labour relations, trade unions, personnel, fringe benefits, occupational hazards, and related subjects is the *Work Related Abstracts*, which is not online. There are databases that cover labour relations such as the BNA *Labor Reporter*, which concentrates on labour court cases and arbitration awards, and the PAIS *Bulletin*, which emphasizes the public affairs and governmental perspectives. Your question may be answered best by searching the *Work Related Abstracts* volumes in hard copy.

2. Do the databases provide the kind of information you require? You may be searching for sources for statistics whereas the databases treating the subject emphasize descriptive and analytic sources.

3. Do they go back far enough? Most databases emphasize the most current information. Databases tend not to go back beyond the period in the late 1970s when the loading of

periodical indexes online began. Some databases drop sources from earlier years. Therefore, for historical research you have to use hard copy for the most part.

4. Would another source (textbook, abstract journal, encyclopedia, library catalogue, telephone call) be better or cheaper? It will certainly be cheaper, and often faster, if the question requires a brief reply.

5. Would an online search be a worthwhile preliminary step even though it could not provide the full answer? You can answer this question only after experience with online searching.

Chapter 2

Catalogues and How to Use Them

What is a catalogue?

A catalogue is a record of the publications the library holds in its collection. It guides you to the specific publication you are looking for.

How many forms of catalogues are there?

Catalogues come in four forms:

1. card catalogues, in which each card represents a separate publication;
2. book catalogues, in which sometimes the entries are printed and other times the cards from the card catalogue are photocopied;
3. microfilm catalogues, which can be used with a microform viewer; and
4. online catalogues, which are seen on a computer terminal screen and operated by a keyboard.

What is your object in consulting the catalogues?

First, you want to see if the library has the particular book you are looking for as well as any other books on the subject you are researching.

   Second, to retrieve the book or books from the library stacks, you must make out a request slip provided by the library by printing the name of the author, title, and classmark or call number given in the catalogue.

The following sections describe how to use the card catalogue, dictionary catalogue, microform catalogue, and online catalogue. Although the online catalogue has largely superseded the older catalogues, it follows the catalogue rules established in the old card catalogues and can best be understood by examining the catalogued cards.

CARD CATALOGUES

Card catalogues are arranged or filed alphabetically by author, subject, and title. For example, for an author named James Finance, all the books by him would be entered in the card catalogue on cards each containing his name and then the title of one of his books, as follows:

Finance, James, 1921–1970.
  Country talk ...

Behind the books written by James Finance are books he has compiled, edited, or co-authored, for example:

Finance, James, 1921–1970, ed.
  Diamond, Alex, 1912–1960.
    The Jubilee years ...

Next come cards for books about James Finance – that is, biographies, reminiscences, and critical works:

Finance, James , 1921–1970
  Jackson, Abel, 1930
    Jimmie Finance, my old pal ...

or

Finance, James, 1921–1970.
    Addison, Joseph, 1926
        The Narrative style of James Finance ...

Following these are cards for books by other authors named Finance such as 'Finance, Zeke,' and then cards with the subject heading FINANCE, followed by cards on which the subject heading is regionalized, that is, FINANCE – FRANCE. Finally, come publications with the title Finance, such as the periodical *Finance* (London) v. 1 no. 1 – May 1950–.

Filing Quirks

Remember that titles are filed after subject headings; otherwise, you may become lost in the thousands of subject-heading cards and think the library does not have the periodical you want. By remembering this arrangement –author, subject, title – you can find your way through the catalogue with ease.

Three simple filing rules will help you locate books in the catalogue:

1. Cards are filed word by word not letter by letter: 'New York,' for example, follows 'New Haven' and precedes 'New Zealand,' but all three precede 'Newport' and 'Newspaper.'
2. Cards with abbreviated capital letters standing for companies or institutions, such as IBM, are found at the beginning of the file for each letter – that is, IBM comes at the beginning of the I's, preceding 'Iago,' for example.
3. In some catalogues 'Mc' (as in 'McNab') is filed as if it were 'Mac' (as in 'MacNab').

Locating Series Volumes or Other Parts of Works

Analyzed Monograph Series

It is important to know how to find a monograph published in a series because you encounter these series often in the most ele-

Fig. 2.1

Write on slip words underlined
and class mark –

Churchill, Winston Leonard Spencer, 1874–   **YFXC**

> **Roosevelt,Franklin Delano** *32d. pres. U.S.* 1882
> ... Address of President Roosevelt, December 29, 1940.
> President Roosevelt's message to Congress, January 6, 1941.
> Prime Minister Churchill's address to the Italian people, De-
> cember 23, 1940. Economic relations between the Americas,
> by Mordecai Ezekiel... New York city, Carnegie endowment
> for international peace, Division of intercource and education
> [1941]
>> 3 p. l., 65–155 p. fold. maps, diagrs. 19½^{cm}. (International concil -
>> iation...February, 1941, no.367)
>> Bibliography:p. 152–155.
>> 1. U.S. – Defenses. 2. American republics. 3. U.S. – Relations
>> (general) with Spanish America. 4. Spanish America – Relations
>> (general) with U.S. I. Churchill, Winston Leonard Spencer,
>> 1874–   II.*Ezekiel, Mordecai, 1899–
>> Library of Congress JX1907.A8 no.367 41-5600
>>   (341.6082) 353.03

mentary research, and library catalogues index them in different ways.

First, the American Library Association defines a series as 'A number of separate works, usually related to one another in subject or otherwise, issued in succession, normally by the same publishers and in uniform style, with a collective title which generally appears at the head of the title page, on the half-title, or on the cover.'

Unnumbered volumes in a monograph series are catalogued as though they were published individually. Numbered volumes in a monograph series issued by a corporate body or institution, however, are given separate catalogue entries yet kept as part of the series. The cataloguer provides a separate card under the author for a particular monograph in a series. For example, under Sir Winston Churchill, we find a monograph he co-authored with Franklin Roosevelt and Mordecai Ezekiel (Figure 2.1). (Cards for this monograph are also filed under Roosevelt and Ezekiel.)

Information required when requesting this monograph will

Fig. 2.2

```
                                                          M–11
                                                          5208
    CONFERENCE BOARD, INC.
       Reports.
    New York.                    v.                    28cm.

       CURRENT ISSUES AVAILABLE IN ECONOMICS DIVISION
       FULL RECORD OF HOLDINGS IN CENTRAL SERIAL RECORD
       Irregular.

    1. Business--Per. and soc. publ.--U.S.
    NN S 3.72 e OSs CSRs PCs, 1s SLs Es, 1s P(2), 1 (U1s,LC1s,X1s)
```

vary from library to library. In the New York Public Research Libraries, you would follow the instructions in the top right-hand corner of the card: 'Write on slip words underlined and class-mark' *only*. Thus, you would write: 'International conciliation Feb 1941 no 367, YFXC.'

If the cataloguer had not analysed this monograph, you would have to find its number from another source (e.g., CBI) and look it up in the library catalogue under the series '*International Conciliation*, No.1–.'

Some institutions issue their own indexes to the monographic series they publish. These are kept on the reference shelves. For instance, the Conference Board, Inc., periodically publishes a *Cumulative Index* to its publications, which lists the publications under subject, author, and title of monograph, and sometimes by series. The card in the catalogue looks like the one in Figure 2.2.

After you find the number of the report you want in the *Cumulative Index*, your request slip should look like Figure 2.3.

Possessive Series

When using the library catalogues, take care to request a monograph series in the correct way. For example, see the catalogue

Fig. 2.3

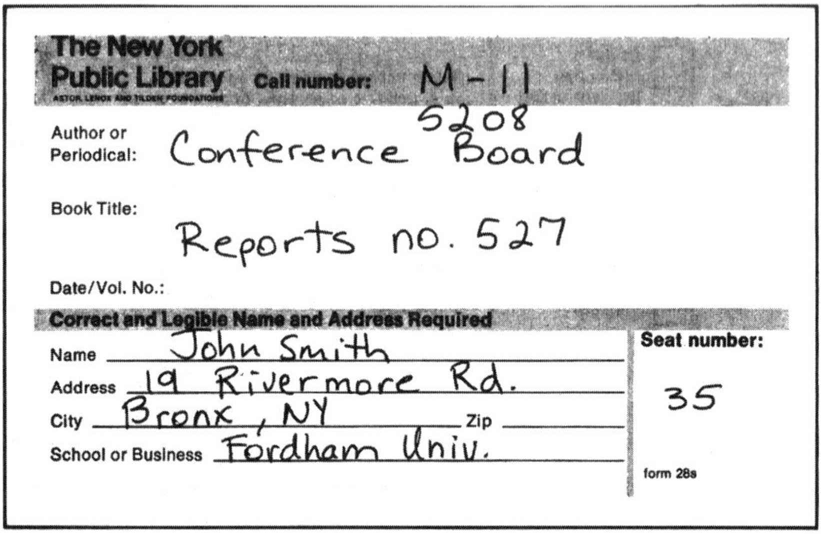

The New York Public Library
ASTOR, LENOX AND TILDEN FOUNDATIONS
Call number: M-11 5208

Author or Periodical: Conference Board

Book Title: Reports no. 527

Date/Vol. No.:

Correct and Legible Name and Address Required

Name: John Smith

Address: 19 Rivermore Rd.

City: Bronx, NY Zip:

School or Business: Fordham Univ.

Seat number: 35

form 28s

entry for a *Farmers' Bulletin* issued by the U.S. Department of Agriculture (Figure 2.4).

Note that the *Farmers' Bulletin* series and the volume number of this particular *Bulletin* are in parentheses. Although it is not underlined, you would fill out your request slip as shown in Figure 2.5.

In other cases the cataloguer can help you find the correct entry by underlining it, as in the example from the NYPL *Dictionary Catalog, 1911–1971* (Figure 2.6).

Series within a Series

In the library catalogues you sometimes encounter publications catalogued with two numbered series. The cataloguer indicates the more important series, or the chief series, by underlining it on the card, noting the subseries in parentheses.

As in Chapter 1, we will use examples from the New York Public Library. In Figure 2.7a,b, from the NYPL *Dictionary Catalog,*

Fig. 2.4

VPZ

McGrew, T.F.
Turkeys: standard varieties and management. Washington: Gov.Prtg.Off., 1904. 40p. illus. 8°. (United States. Agriculture Dept. Farmers' bull.200.)

1. Turkey.
N.Y.P.L. January 23, 1913.

Fig. 2.5

The New York Public Library
ASTOR, LENOX AND TILDEN FOUNDATIONS
Call number: VPZ

Author or Periodical: United States Agriculture Dept.
Book Title: Farmers' Bulletin # 200
Date/Vol. No.:

Correct and Legible Name and Address Required

Name Mary Jackson
Address 31 Main St.
City NY NY Zip
School or Business Allardyce

Seat number: 72

form 28s

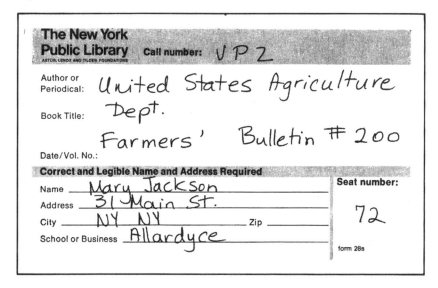

Fig. 2.6

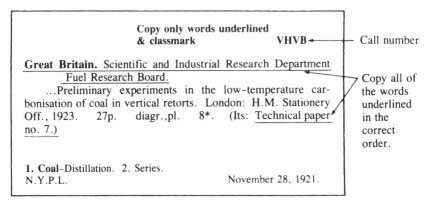

 shows the catalogue card reproduced below:

> **Copy only words underlined**
> **& classmark**   **VHVB** ◄——— Call number
>
> **Great Britain.** Scientific and Industrial Research Department
>   Fuel Research Board.
>   ...Preliminary experiments in the low–temperature car-
> bonisation of coal in vertical retorts. London: H.M. Stationery
> Off., 1923.   27p.   diagr.,pl.   8*.   (Its: Technical paper
> no. 7.)
>
> ← Copy all of the words underlined in the correct order.
>
> 1. **Coal**-Distillation. 2. Series.
> N.Y.P.L.   November 28, 1921.

1911–1971, we can see two main entries under Espinas, Georges. The first is an author entry, but we are instructed to order the volumes under the monograph series '*Société d'histoire du droit des pays flamands, picards et wallons. Bibliothèque.*' The four volumes of the title in the series are numbered 7, 9, 16, and 20. The second card is a series entry – actually a possessive series. The series on the first card is noted on this card as well, but this time the cataloguer regards it as the lesser series and reverses its word order.

When you do as the card asks, your request slip is returned and marked 'verify.' Could the cataloguer have underlined the wrong series? You check the catalogue under the series 'Espinas, Georges. Les Origines de l'association' but you do not find it. You do not find the series 'Bibliothèque de la société d'histoire du droit ...' either. You then check for the series '*Société d'histoire du droit* ...,' which you find. You request Espinas' two volumes on the origins of the law of associations, as in Figure 2.8.

You receive the two volumes. You have overcome the cataloguer's mistake, and have been reminded how important it is to be alert. Always double-check and think of alternative approaches to your search when you encounter any difficulties.

Fig. 2.7a In this case, the series vol.20 corresponds to fasicule 4 of the title.
You request the volumes by series.

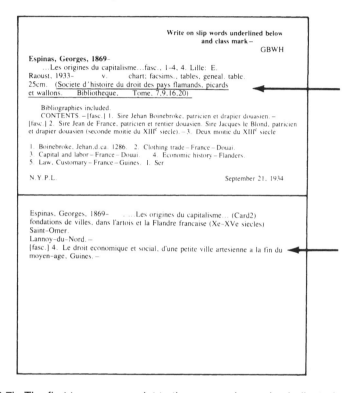

Fig. 2.7b The first two arrows point to the possessive series indicated wrongly
by the cataloguer. The third arrow points to the true series.

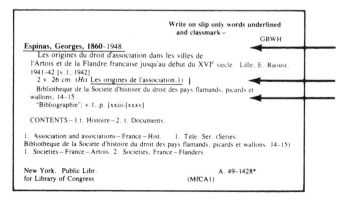

Fig. 2.8

The New York Public Library
ASTOR, LENOX AND TILDEN FOUNDATIONS

Call number: G B WH

Author or Periodical: Societé d'histoire du

Book Title: droit des pays flamands, picards et wallons

Date/Vol. No.: Bibliothèque t. 14 + 15

Correct and Legible Name and Address Required

Name Mary Jackson

Address 3U Main St.

City NY NY   Zip 10007

School or Business Allardyce Inc

Seat number: 72

form 28s

Indexed Book Sets

Another way of cataloguing a monograph series is to 'index' or list the monographs below the description of the entry. This practice is reserved for a short series of a few volumes, referred to as a *book set*. The individual title of each volume is listed under the main entry in order of the volume numbers. A limited series of monographs by different authors, published under one distinctive series title, could be treated in this way. More common are volumes in a series by one author, such as those of Randolph Churchill in the example in Figure 2.9.

As the '*R' indicates, these volumes are on the reference room shelves in NYPL. Sometimes secondary source material is elevated to primary status by the significance of its subject matter. (Similarly, two or three editions of any encyclopedia are kept on the reference room shelves because significant information in the earlier editions is not found in the latest edition.) In this case, we note that the entry remains open (i.e., '1966– '). We expect more volumes to appear, as the last volume covers Winston Churchill's

Fig. 2.9

Churchill, Randolph Spencer, 1911-1968. Winston
S. Churchill, by Randolph S. Churchill.
Illustrated with photographs and maps. Boston,
Houghton Mifflin, 1966- -v. illus., ports. 24 cm.
FULL RECORD OF HOLDINGS IN CENTRAL
SERIAL RECORD. Companion vols., containing
documents relating to vol. 2, were completed by Martin
Gilbert. Vol. 3-4 by Martin Gilbert. CONTENTS. - v. 1.
Youth, 1874-1900. - v. 2. Young statesman, 1901-1914. -
Companion v. 2. 1901-1911, pts. 1-2. v. 3. The challenge
of war, 1914-1916. - v. 4. The stricken world, 1916-1922.
        NN 73-4229859
                    [*R-AN (Churchill) 73-3100]

Fig. 2.10

STEWART,ALEXANDER TURNEY,1803-1876
                        Copy only words underlined
                        & classmark—
                                    HAER

RESSEQUE, HARRY E.
     The folklore of A.T. Stewart. (IN: New York folklore
quarterly. Cooperstown.   22cm.   v.18, no. 2 (summer, 1962)
p. 125-141)

     Bibliography, p. 140-141.

1. Stewart, Alexander Turney, 1803-1876.
NN R 8.63 p/j OI (PC)1 (E)1 (LC2, X1)

life only to 1922. On the open reference shelves, a discrete space
is left for the continuations.

Catalogue Indexing of Magazine Articles

Before the 1960s, when periodical indexes had not yet appeared
for almost every subject field, librarians indexed magazine articles and essays in books under the author as main entry in the
catalogue. This is generally not done today (see Figure 2.10).

Fig. 2.11

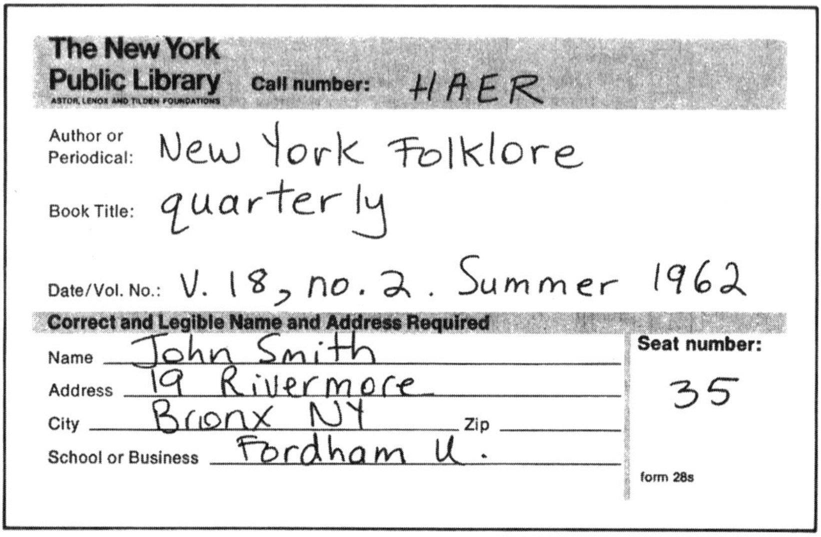
The New York Public Library
ASTOR, LENOX AND TILDEN FOUNDATIONS
Call number: HAER

Author or Periodical: New York Folklore

Book Title: quarterly

Date/Vol. No.: V. 18, no. 2. Summer 1962

Correct and Legible Name and Address Required

Name John Smith

Address 19 Rivermore

City Bronx NY Zip

School or Business Fordham U.

Seat number: 35

form 28s

On the request slip you write only the title of the periodical, the date, and the call number (Figure 2.11). But remember to record the pages in your own notes.

Requesting a Work from the Catalogue

First you fill out a request slip by printing the name of the author, the title, and the call number. Thus, if you wanted the hypothetical book about James Finance mentioned earlier, you would write:

Jackson, Abel
  Jimmie Finance

and then fill in the call number from the top right-hand corner of the card.

Let us suppose that you want to request a book by Sir Winston Churchill, which you found in the catalogue under Churchill's name or under a subject heading (Figure 2.12 a,b). You fill out

Fig. 2.12a

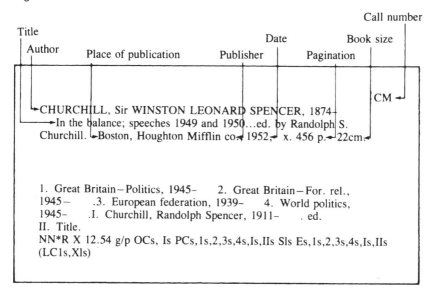

Fig. 2.12b

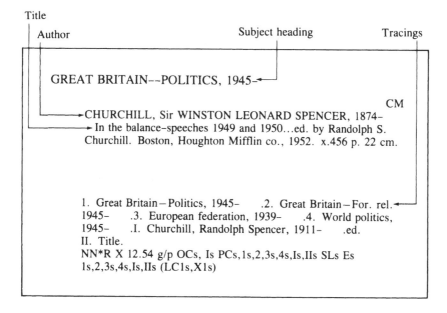

Fig. 2.13

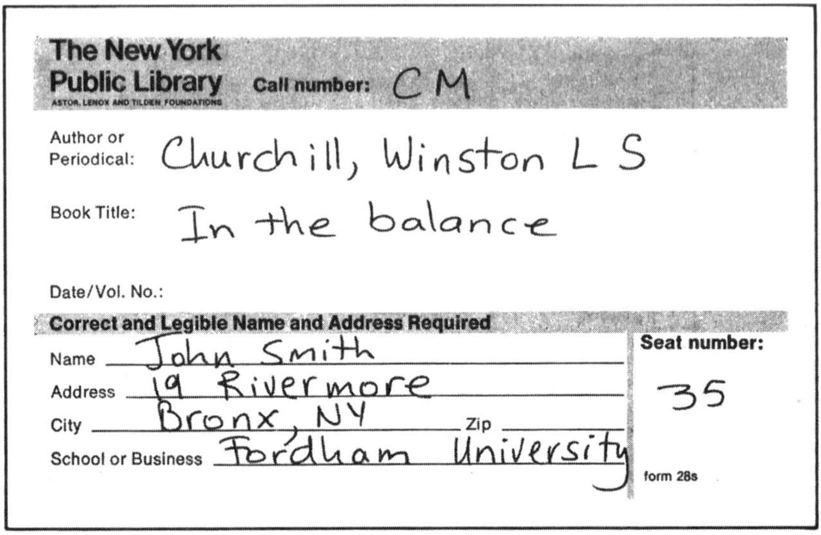

The New York Public Library
ASTOR, LENOX AND TILDEN FOUNDATIONS
Call number: CM

Author or Periodical: Churchill, Winston L S

Book Title: In the balance

Date/Vol. No.:

Correct and Legible Name and Address Required

Name John Smith
Address 19 Rivermore
City Bronx, NY Zip
School or Business Fordham University

Seat number: 35

form 28s

the request slip as follows: Write down the call number,[1] the author, and the title as they appear on the card (see Figure 2.13). If there is more than one volume, designate the volume you want, such as 'Vol. 2 only,' or 'all vols.'

How do you request a periodical? Suppose you want the periodical *Finance*: the card in the catalogue looks like Figure 2.14. Thus, you will fill out a request slip, which looks like Figure 2.15. Always write the call number, title, and the month and year or volume number of a periodical on your request slip.

Let us take another look at the catalogue entry for the periodical *Finance* shown in Figure 2.14. Note that it is marked 'v. 72–date; 1957–date.' This means that the entry starts with volume 72, published in 1957, and the library contains all subsequent issues to 'date,' meaning to the present (see below about confirming the 'full record'). These issues can be retrieved from the stacks by

1 This designates where the publication is shelved in the library.

Fig. 2.14

```
                                                                    M–10
                                                                    1072
FINANCE: all the news of the hire of the dollar.  v. 72–
    date: 1957–date
    Chicago, Finance pub. corp.      v.       illus., ports.
    29cm.
            FULL RECORD OF HOLDINGS IN CENTRAL SERIAL RECORD
    CURRENT IN ECONOMICS DIVISION
    Monthly.
    Began publication in Sept. 1941 with title:  Finance and the Chicago
banker (not in the library) and until July, 1942, continued the numbering of the
Chicago banker. In Aug., 1942, assumed
                                        (Continued)
NN R 7.63 p/jOSs, Is, II PCs, 1s, 2s, II SLs Es, 1s, 2s, II Ps (2s) 1s, 2s,
II (U1s, 1C1s, X1s)
```

```
FINANCE:  all the news of the hire of the dollar.
            (Cont.)

the v. numbering of another earlier publication, the Financial review.
    One issue each year includes the section: Net worths of the leading
underwriters.




1.  Banks and banking--Per. and soc. publ.--U.S.  2.  Securities--Per. and
soc. publ.--U.S.  I.  Finance and the Chicago banker.  II.  Finance; all the news
of the hire of the dollar. Net worths of the leading underwriters.
```

filling out a request slip in the ordinary way. Issues of the current
year, however, as the card informs you, are kept on the current
shelves in the Economic Division (the division's name has been
changed to the SIBL reference library since the card was
printed); hence, you must ask the librarian at SIBL for them.

For the years before 1957, the card merely informs you of the
history of the publication, but it does not say the library has those
early titles. Look at the card again. It informs you that the period-

Fig. 2.15

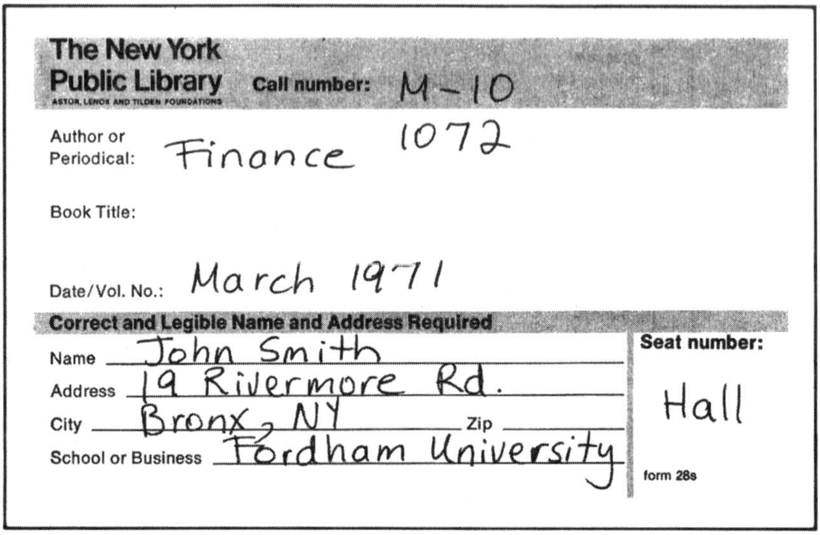

The New York
Public Library   Call number: $M-10$
ASTOR, LENOX AND TILDEN FOUNDATIONS

Author or
Periodical: Finance   1072

Book Title:

Date/Vol. No.:   March 1971

Correct and Legible Name and Address Required

Name   John Smith   Seat number:
Address 19 Rivermore Rd.
City   Bronx, NY   Zip   Hall
School or Business Fordham University
                                                       form 28s

ical *Finance* began publication in September 1941 under the title *Finance and the Chicago Banker*, which the library did *not* collect (see p. 20 for ways of locating copies). This earlier publication apparently took over the periodical *Chicago Banker*, whose volume numbering it continued; therefore, for issues published before September 1941, you would have to look in the catalogue under the *Chicago Banker*. The card also informs you that in August 1942, the *Finance and the Chicago Banker* took over or amalgamated with the *Financial Review*, of which the library has issues published prior to 1942.

Last, stamped across the card are the words FULL RECORD OF HOLDINGS IN CENTRAL SERIAL RECORD. This means that the recording of the issues of the periodical *Finance* received by the library are kept in a central location, which the librarian may telephone or reach through a computer monitor. Before library procedures were automated, cards recording the years of the periodical (called *holding cards*) were filed in the catalogue behind the main card and kept up-to-date by filers. At the NYPL,

Fig. 2.16

```
                                                              *SYB
CALGARY, Alberta.  Comptroller.
   ...Financial statistics...and statement of net general
debt and borrowing power.
      FULL RECORD OF HOLDINGS IN CENTRAL SERIAL RECORD
[Calgary, 1926–                                        21½ cm.

   Annual.
   Title varies slightly.


   1.  Finance – Canada – Calgary.

                                              PUB. DOC. CAT.

N.Y.P.L.                                         June 29, 1937
```

these holding cards have been removed and the information on them has been fed into a computer storage terminal so that a reference librarian can ascertain the extent of the holdings within seconds on a computer monitor. If the item has been converted to the online catalogue, you can call up the screen indicating the library's holdings by year and issue of the periodical.

One final point to be made regarding periodical titles: you should know that some periodicals are entered in the catalogue by the name of the institution or government agency that issues them – for example, 'Ford Foundation. *Newsletter*,' or 'U.S. Treasury Dept. *Monthly Bulletin*.'

If you request a book by a government agency or institution, the agency is listed as the author, thus (see Figure 2.16): It is logical to state the place first: 'Calgary, Alberta,' followed by its government agency: 'Comptroller.' You can fill out the request slip by entering 'Calgary, Alberta, Comptroller' as the author, as in Figure 2.17.

Fig. 2.17

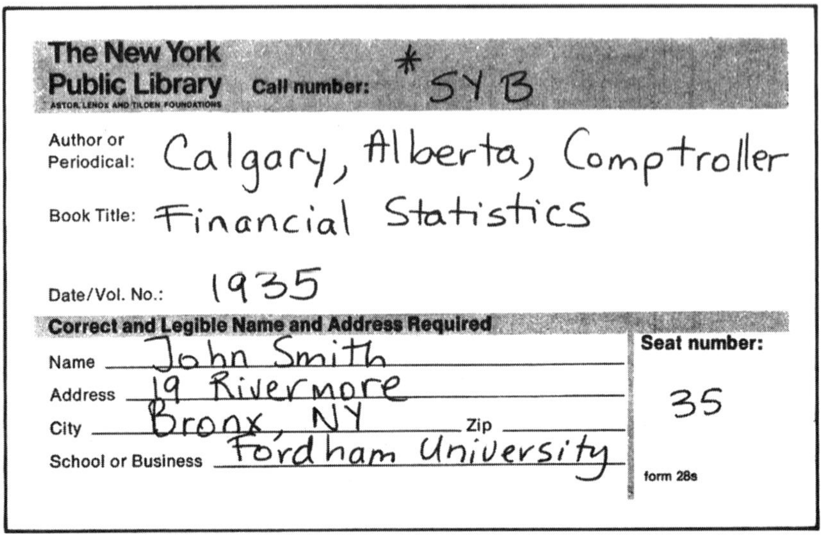

The New York Public Library
ASTOR, LENOX AND TILDEN FOUNDATIONS
Call number: *SYB

Author or Periodical: Calgary, Alberta, Comptroller

Book Title: Financial Statistics

Date/Vol. No.: 1935

Correct and Legible Name and Address Required

Name: John Smith

Address: 19 Rivermore

City: Bronx, NY Zip

School or Business: Fordham University

Seat number: 35

form 28s

BOOK CATALOGUES

In every research and university library you will find a section holding the multivolume book catalogues of the important research libraries of the world. They are useful when doing historical research. Many but not all of them have been converted over the years to the libraries' online catalogues. One of the most useful and most used catalogues of this group is the NYPL *Dictionary Catalog of the Research Libraries, 1911–71.* It serves as a good example for the many large libraries that have not converted their older collection to online.

NYPL Dictionary Catalog of the Research Libraries, 1911–71

The Dictionary Catalog, 1911–71, consists of reproductions of the cards from NYPL's entire main card catalogue once shelved in the central catalogue room of the General Reference Division in 800 volumes; thus, it catalogues all the books, periodicals, and pamphlets catalogued by the library before 1972, when the card catalogue was closed. You will find these volumes in almost every research and university library. In 1972 the library began automating new accessions into an online catalogue and printed for a few years an automated book catalogue, which printed the computerized entries, for those readers unwilling to use the online system. When the card catalogue was closed, many shelves of publications for years past were waiting to be catalogued; they were eventually catalogued in the online or automated catalogues, so that for works published before 1972 that were not in the main *Dictionary Catalog, 1911–71*, you must check the online catalogue.

The online catalogue now contains most of the library's holdings, even many of those before 1972, as the library has been steadily processing those entries from the *Dictionary Catalog, 1911–71*, into the online catalogue. All research libraries are converting their old catalogue entries as finances permit.

Automated Book Catalogues

Some libraries maintain printed automated book catalogues while others have discarded them because they were simply printed versions of the online catalogue. Automated book catalogue entries, however, provide you with a unique opportunity to examine the look of the entries you will see on the online catalogue and thereby serve as illustrations of the format and errors you will encounter online. Every library online catalogue system provides a full display of the entry.

Figure 2.18a shows a sample column from one of the volumes, with comments to help you decipher it.

Let us suppose you are looking for works by Sir Winston Churchill, the British prime minister during the Second World War. The first name on the page (Figure 2.18a) reads 'CHURCHILL, WINSTON, 1871–1947.' Be careful. This is not the Winston Churchill you want; it is his American cousin. The next name entry is 'Churchill, Winston J., 1940– ' – the wrong man, again. The third name entry, 'Churchill, Winston Leonard

Fig. 2.18a

CHURCHILL, WINSTON, 1871-1947.
Barker, Elisabeth. Churchill and Eden at war /.
London , 1978. 346 p. ;   NN 79-4724128   LC
79-314303   [JFD 79-11149]

Schneider, Robert W. Novelist to a generation .
Bowling Green, Ohio , c1976. xvl, 333 p. :   NN
76-4895022   LC 76-4643   [JFE 77-75]

The scrapbooks of Winston Churchill, American
novelist and politician. [v. p., 1899-1912] 30 v.
NN 79-4633151   [*Z-2980]

Churchill, Winston J., 1940- Running in place, by
Winston J. Churchill. New York, G. Braziller
[1973] 218 p. 22 cm.   NN 73-4275325   LC
72-92832   [JFD 73-6526]

Churchill, Winston Leonard Spencer, Sir, 1874-
1965.
[Works]
The collected works of Sir Winston Churchill.
Centenary limited edition. [London] Library of
Imperial History [1973- -v. maps, ports. 25 cm.
FULL RECORD OF HOLDINGS IN CENTRAL
SERIAL RECORD. Half title: The first collected
works of Sir Winston Churchill. Issued in slipcases.
3000 numbered sets. NYPL set, no. 2052.
CONTENTS. - v. 1. My early life. My African
journey. - v. 2. The story of the Malakand Field
Force. - v. 3. The River War. - v. 4. The Boer war:
London to Ladysmith via Pretoria. Ian Hamilton's
march. - v. 5. Savrola. - v. 6. Lord Randolph
Churchill. - v. 7. Mr. Brodrick's army and other
speeches. - v. 8-12. The world crisis, pt. 1-5. - v. 13.
Thoughts and adventures. - v. 14-15. Marlborough, v.
1-2. - v. 16. Great contemporaries. - v. 17. Arms and
the covenant. - v. 18. Step by step, 1936-1939. - v.
19-21. War speeches, v. 1-3. - v. 22-27. The Second
World War: v. 1 The Gathering storm. - 2. Their
finest hour. - 3. The grand alliance. - v. The hinge of
fate. - 5. Closing the ring. - 6. Triump and tragedy.
Epilogue. - v. 28, 30. Post-war speeches - 1. The
sinews of peace. Europe unite. - 3. Stemming the tide.
The unwritten alliance. - v. 33-34. A history of the
English speaking peoples. [v. 35-38?] Collected essays
of Sir Winston Churchill, v. 1-4: v. 1. Churchill and
War. v. 2. Churchill and politics. v. 3. Churchill and
peole. v. 4 Churchill ar large.   NN 74-4958680
                    [8-*ITG (Gt. Br.: 1974) 74-1241]

Spencer, Sir, 1876–1965,' is undoubtedly the man you want. This
entry in bold type is called the author entry.

Cataloguers try to make an author entry as complete as possible, for the researcher's convenience. For instance, here are the
names of Churchills who are authors in the order in which they
are listed in the catalogue:

Fig. 2.18b

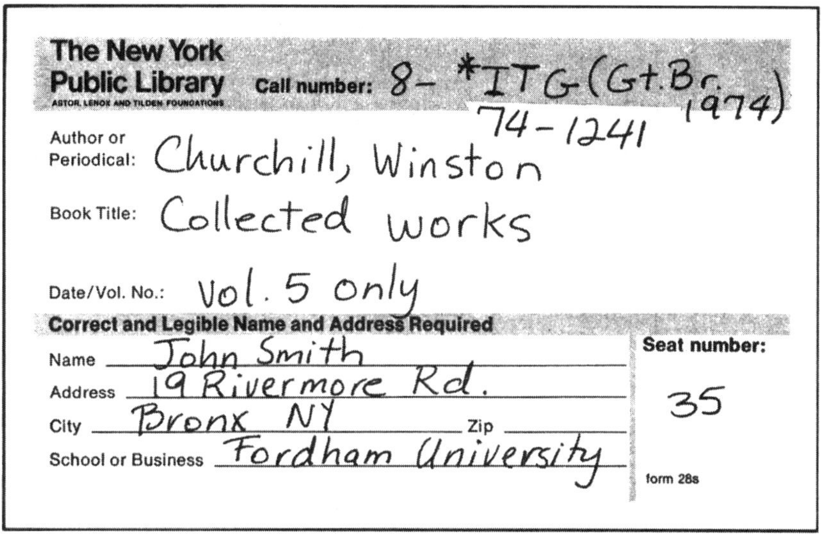

The New York Public Library Call number: 8- *ITG (Gt. Br. 1974) 74-1241
ASTOR, LENOX AND TILDEN FOUNDATIONS

Author or Periodical: Churchill, Winston

Book Title: Collected works

Date/Vol. No.: Vol. 5 only

Correct and Legible Name and Address Required

Name John Smith

Address 19 Rivermore Rd.

City Bronx NY Zip

School or Business Fordham University

Seat number: 35

form 28s

Churchill, Randolph Spencer, 1874–
Churchill, Winston, 1871–1947
Churchill, Winston J., 1940–
Churchill, Winston Leonard Spencer, Sir, 1874–1965
Churchill, Winston Spencer, 1940–

In our example, note that the first entry, 'CHURCHILL, WINSTON, 1871–1947,' is in capital letters. This is a subject entry. It heads a list of books about an American novelist, Winston Churchill.

We note that the first main entry, 'Barker, Elizabeth,' is followed on the same line by the title *Churchill and Eden at War,* which is a surprising role for an American novelist. We conclude that the cataloguer made a mistake; the entry should come under the subject heading for Sir Winston Churchill. This is confirmed by inspecting the books, thus demonstrating the fallibility of catalogues. This is a useful lesson for the researcher.

The second and third entries under the subject heading

appear to be correctly listed under the novelist, Winston Churchill. Note that the third entry is by title, *The scrapbooks* ... in 30 volumes.

In each case, the call number is in boldface in brackets below and on the right side of the entries (see Figure 2.18a). (In the card catalogue, you will recall, the call number appeared in the upper right-hand corner.)

The first entry under 'Churchill, Winston Leonard Spencer, Sir,' is his *Collected Works*. To get the correct volume, you need to describe it with exactness on your request slip. For instance, if you wish to read Sir Winston Churchill's only novel, *Savrola*, you must write, 'Vol. 5 only' (Figure 2.18b).

You do not need to worry about writing the correct author and title from these computerized entries because each call number is unique to the book it represents. For instance, in our example (Figure 2.19a), at the first entry, Churchill is joint author with Franklin Roosevelt. You may be confused as to the main author entry, Churchill or Roosevelt. In this case you need write only the call number on the request slip, although it is preferable to fill in the author and short title for verification purposes (Fig 2.19b).

Lower in the column, the catalogue lists works about Sir Winston Churchill under the subject heading 'CHURCHILL, WINSTON LEONARD SPENCER, SIR, 1874–1965.'

Interim List

A later, automated book catalogue called the NYPL Research Libraries' *Interim List: Index* of publications catalogued after 1981, which also was discarded some years ago, provides us with an example of the library's attempt to add subject tracings to the computerized entries. This experiment led to the listing of subject headings in entries in the online catalogue, which in most instances can be pulled up on the screen by checking tabs such as 'full' for full description or 'long' for a complete display. In order to make the main entry clearer, each main entry in this interim catalogue was preceded by an asterisk (see Figure 2.20).

Fig. 2.19a

(joint author) Roosevelt, Franklin Delano, Pres. U. S., 1882-1945. Roosevelt and Churchill. New York, 1975. xvi, 805 p. NN 75-4584665 LC 74-14854 **[JFE 75-2679]**

Two messages to Poland. [n. p., 1942?] folder ([6] p.) NN 76-4213864 **[*XM-6419]**

Winston S. Churchill: his complete speeches, 1897-1963. Edited by Robert Phodes James. New York, Chelsea House Publishers, 1974. 8 v. (xvi, 8917 p.). illus. 25 cm. NN 74-4703326 **[*R-CM 74-3680]**

Young Winston's wars; the original despatches of Winston S. Churchill, war correspondent, 1897-1900. Edited and with an introd. and notes by Frederick Woods. London, L. Cooper [1972] xxviii, 350 p. ports., maps. 23 cm. NN 73-4295961 **[JFD 73-1499]**

CHURCHILL, WINSTON LEONARD SPENCER, SIR, 1874-1965.
Aigner, Dietrich. Winston Churchill . Göttingen [1975] 152 p., [4] leaves of plates : NN 77-4444118 LC 75-507474 **[JFC 77-1565]**

Fig. 2.19b

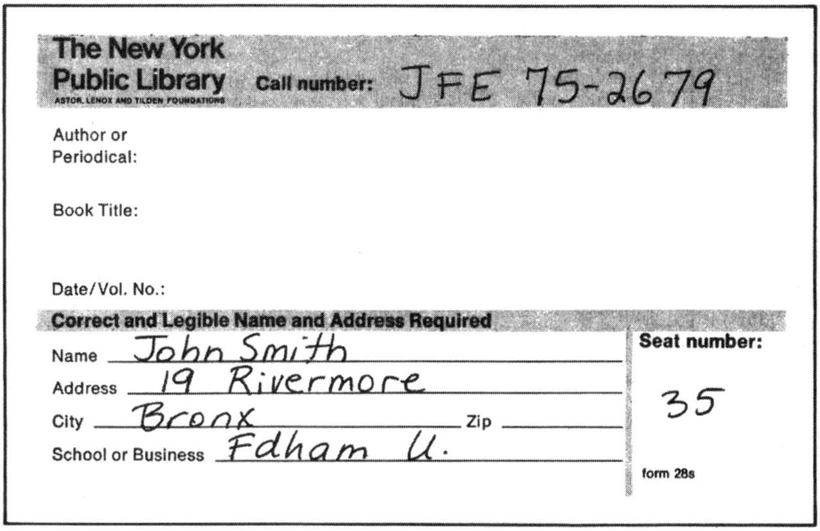
The New York Public Library
ASTOR, LENOX AND TILDEN FOUNDATIONS
Call number: JFE 75-2679

Author or Periodical:

Book Title:

Date/Vol. No.:

Correct and Legible Name and Address Required

Name John Smith
Address 19 Rivermore
City Bronx Zip
School or Business Fdham U.

Seat number: 35

form 28s

Fig. 2.20

> Churchill, Winston Leonard Spencer, Sir, 1874-
> 1965.
> *Statesmanship : — Carolina Academic Press,
> c1981. viii, 279 p.
>   Reg. no.: 0071711
>   **Call no.: JFE 83-617**
> Blood, sweat, and tears, — G. P. Putnam's sons
> [c1941] x, 462 p. front. (port.)
>   Reg. no.: 0059470
>   **Call no.: JFD 82-2948**
> The unrelenting struggle; — [1st ed.] — Little,
> Brown, 1942. ix, 371 p.
>   Reg. no.: 0061181
>   **Call no.: JFD 82-3547**
>
> **CHURCHILL, WINSTON LEONARD**
> **SPENCER, SIR, 1874-1965.**
> *Callahan, Raymond.
> Churchill : — Scholarly Resources, 1984. xiii, 293
> p.
>   Reg. no.: 0190911
>   **Call no.: JFE 84-2307**
>
> *Seldon, Anthony.
> Churchill's Indian summer : — Hodder &
> Stoughton, 1981. xvii, 667 p., [4] leaves of plates :
> ill., ports.
>   Reg. no.: 0026240
>   **Call no.: JFE 82-54**

Therefore, the first entry under 'Churchill, Winston ...,' which is *'Statesmanship,'* is both title and main entry, whereas the second entry in the column, which is not asterisked, indicates that 'Churchill, Winston ...' is the author entry and the main entry to a book entitled *Blood, sweat and tears.* The call number is below the bibliographic description. Further down the column is the subject heading in capital letters: 'CHURCHILL, WINSTON LEONARD SPENCER, SIR, 1874–1965.' Below it, an asterisk by the author entries indicates that they are the main entries.

Just above the call number for all the entries in these volumes, the term 'Reg. no.,' for registration number, appears. This number refers to an entry in a set of volumes called *Interim List: Register,* which accompanied the *Interim List: Index* volumes. Every entry had a registration number. These registration numbers were listed numerically in the *Register* volumes. For instance, the registration number for the book by Seldon is 0026240. Turning to the number in the *Register,* you find that the entry is given a fully bibliographic citation including tracings (see Figure 2.21).

Fig. 2.21

```
0026240
 *Seldon, Anthony.
  Churchill's Indian summer : the Conservative
  government, 1951-55 / Anthony Seldon. -- London :
  Hodder & Stoughton, 1981. xvii, 667 p., [4] leaves
  of plates : ill., ports. ; 24 cm.
   Bibliography: p. 627-645.
   Includes index.
   LCCN:   81181385
   1. Great Britain -- Politics and government --
   1945-1964. 2. Churchill, Winston Leonard Spencer,
   -- Sir, -- 1874-1965.
       Call no.: [JFE 82-54]
```

Carlyle System

The computer catalogue known as the Carlyle System was based on the *Index* and *Register* format described above. You can call to the screen the *Index* citation of a publication to get its call number. If you want the full bibliographic citation and the subject-heading tracings, you can call its *Register* to the screen. This was the way in which brief and full descriptions were developed for online catalogues. You, as a reader, simply type out the instructions on the screen, press the command or 'return' or 'send' key, and a monitor displays the call number and a description of the publication. You can then call up a fuller description complete with subject headings such as for the fifth item displayed. A full citation (display full 5) to be printed (Print full 5) is shown in Figure 2.22.

The modifying command is important. *Modifying commands* (or *Boolean operators*) are the words *AND, OR,* and *AND NOT,* followed by the type of search (such as author, title, or subject) and then the words that modify your original request. For example:

AND title: information processing
OR subject: solar
AND NOT subject: environment

AND narrows your search to items that contain both the words in your original search and the words after the modifying command. OR expands or enlarges your search to include items con-

Fig. 2.22

Search request:	F A ARMSTRONG
Items found:	36
Print request:	PRINT FULL 5

Item 5.

AUTHOR	Armstrong, Lilian.
TITLE	Renaissance miniature painters & classical imagery: the Master of the Putti and his Venetian workshop / Lilian Armstrong.
PUBLICATION	London: Harvey Miller, c1981.
DESCRIPTION	viii, 223 p., [5] leaves of plates: ill. (some col.) facsims.; 28 cm.
NOTES	Includes indexes. Bibliography; p. 139-148.
SUBJECTS	1. Master of the Putti, 15th cent. 2. Master of the London Pliny, 15th cent. 3. Illumination of books and manuscripts, Renaissance--Italy--Venice.
CALL NUMBER	JFF 83-126

taining either the words in your original request or those after the modifying command. AND NOT includes items containing the words in your original request, but not the words after the modifying command. For example, (f/t= find title; f/s= find subject):

Type: f/t Mexico and not new and not mayan
Items found: 64
  f/s indians and not mayan and not mexican
Items found: 249
  f/s anthropology and mexico and not new
Items found: 5

Online cataloguing systems allow you to back up or call for full displays by different methods such as calling up windows to the screen by clicking on icons or designated tabs.

Different Cataloguing Arrangements

To this point we have been talking about Dictionary Catalogues in which entries are filed alphabetically. Some libraries use the Divided Catalogue, in which cards for authors and titles are arranged alphabetically in one list and subject cards are listed in a separate alphabetical arrangement. There are variations on this theme – for instance, authors may be separated from titles to form a third catalogue, or works about individuals may be filed with authors' names in a Names catalogue.

The Classified Catalogue arranges works in a logical subject order, placing similar books together, under a numbering system. The Engineering Society's Library in New York City requires you to locate the classification number for a particular subject before you can use the subject card catalogue.

The Dewey Decimal Classification System arranges books by subject number. In the circulating libraries it is used to make it easier for the public to locate books on the open shelves; in the case of research libraries, the public uses either a Dictionary or Divided Catalogue to look up the classification number. Similarly, the U.S. Library of Congress uses a subject numbering classification, but its readers use a Dictionary Catalogue to look up the L.C. call number.

Other Types of Catalogues in Research Libraries

The British Library in London uses large, leather-backed volumes into which are inserted pages with pasted-on, printed bibliographic descriptions of its holdings, with call numbers. These insertions are arranged alphabetically by name. To find books by subject heading you use bound printed volumes for the early periods and microfilm cassettes for after 1970 (see page 175).

The Bibliothèque Nationale in Paris has recorded its holdings in a variety of catalogue forms over the years: in printed book catalogues, card catalogues, and small looseleaf or sheaf catalogues. Periodicals are catalogued in a separate card catalogue. These catalogues are designated by the years of acquisition they cover. Remember, however, that a book published in 1890 may have been acquired by the library in 1950 and will be located through the catalogue covering acquisitions in 1950. See the catalogues of the Bibliothèque Nationale on page 177.

Yale University Library has a variety of catalogues. Its online catalogue is Orbis, in which are found publications catalogued in

1977 and after. Publications before 1977 may be found in the Sterling Memorial Library Card Catalog containing 11,986 drawers, representing over 100 years of cataloguing records for the fourth-largest library in the United States. It contains cards for material in most formats held by most of the libraries in the Yale University Library System represented on a combination of handwritten, half-height cards; typewritten cards; and computer-produced cards. Special catalogues for materials not accessible through Orbis or the SML Card Catalog can be found in the form of handwritten indexes, traditional card format, published book catalogues, or separate database files. For manuscript and archival collections, finding aids have been created. There is a separate online catalogue, Morris, for the Yale University Law Library.

These are the variety of catalogues you can expect to deal with in most large research libraries worldwide. Some of the smaller research libraries have no online catalogue and rely on the card and printed book catalogues. To check publications in Orbis (less than one-half of the library's holdings) over the Internet use http://www.library.yale.edu or simply type the name of the library into one of the search engines.

The catalogues of most large libraries can be found on the Internet (for URLs see pages 20–1).

OPEN-SHELF REFERENCE BOOKS

How do you request books you cannot find in the library catalogues?

If the publication is not in the online catalogue and if you know only the title, you will *not* find the book in Dictionary Catalogs unless the title was considered distinctive. Titles of directories, encyclopedias, and collected readings are considered distinctive and given main entries in preference to their editors or compilers. A book by the famous Sir Winston Churchill, *In the Balance*, was considered to have a distinctive title and given a title added entry. But ordinary books are listed in the catalogue only by the author's names; if you can remember only a title, you should consult other sources to find the author's name. Suppose, for instance, you want to see a novel entitled *Leave Her to Heaven*, and you have forgotten the name of the author; you would proceed to consult the following:

Books in Print (BIP) lists all books currently available from American publishers. Author, title, and subject indexes are published annually. Look in the title index volume of BIP for *Leave Her to Heaven* to find the author. Monthly indexes of books in print, entitled *Forthcoming Books*, announce recently published or about-to-be-published books. *Whittaker's Books of the Month to Come* announces publications in England. If the book you want is not listed in the BIP you may check *Canadian Books in Print* and *British Books in Print*.

You cannot find *Leave Her to Heaven* in BIP, because it is out of print. What do you do next? You turn to a valuable comprehensive source, *The Cumulative Book Index* (CBI), which is a monthly publication listing all books and pamphlets in the English language by author, title, series, and subject heading. It is cumulated quarterly, annually, and every few years. If you have a rough idea of the date of the book, work systematically through volumes covering the period, quickly checking under title. You locate *Leave Her to Heaven* in the CBI volume covering 1943–8 and note its author, Ben Ames Williams. Then you can locate the library call number for the novel by looking in the library catalogue under Williams, Ben Ames.

If you know only the title of a book in a foreign language, you can find the author in the national bibliography published by the foreign country.[2]

How do you request articles in periodicals, newspapers, and books?

Let us suppose you need to research a bibliography of sources such as the following:

---

2 For the titles of national bibliographies, see Vladimir M. Palic, *Government Publications: A Guide to Bibliographic Tools*, 4th ed. (Washington, DC: Library of Congress, 1975).

1. Letelier, Isabel, and Michael Moffit, 'Supporting Repression: Multinational Banks in Chile,' *Race and Class* 20 (Autumn 1978): 111–28. In this case you look for the periodical *Race and Class* in the library catalogue and fill out a request slip with the call number of the periodical, the title of the periodical, and the date of the article only.
2. Jahn, G.R., 'Image of the Railroad in *Anna Karenina*,' *Slavic and East European Journal* 25 (Summer 1981): 1–10. You would use the same procedure as described above.
3. Vicker, Roy, 'In the Middle: Cairo, as Big Recipient of Aid, Heeds Views of both U.S., Saudis …,' *Wall St. Journal* 193 (7 March 1979): 1+. In this case you request the *Wall Street Journal* for 7 March 1979 (which is on microfilm) and look for the article on page 1.
4. Simons, Henry C., 'Unions as Monopolies,' in C. Lowell Harriss, ed., *Selected Readings in Economics* (Englewood Cliffs, NJ: Prentice-Hall, 1958), 195–200. In this case you look in the library catalogue under 'Harriss, C. Lowell, ed.' for the book *Selected Readings* and request it by call number.

How do you find articles on a given subject?

You look in periodical indexes, most of which are issued every two weeks, and cumulated quarterly and annually. There are periodical indexes for almost all subject fields. The most popular are *The Readers' Guide to Periodical Literature* (which indexes articles by author and subject), the Public Affairs Information Service (PAIS) *Bulletin*, the *Applied Science and Technology Index*, and the *Bibliography Index*.

After finding an article in the periodical index, you proceed to find the call number for the periodical in which the article was printed. For example, suppose you have been given citation 2 in the preceding bibliography but could remember only that it concerned Tolstoi's novel *Anna Karenina* and was printed in 1981. You would look in the *Humanities Index* for 1981 under Tolstoi and find the following:

TOLSTOI, Lev Nikolaevich, graf
about
Image of the railroad in Anna Karenina, G.R Jahn
Slavic & E Eur 25: 1–10. Summ '81

You find the full title of the journal in a list of abbreviations in the front of the index volume and then check the library catalogue for that journal's call number.[3]

Suppose you have been given the author and subject of a pamphlet, but you cannot find it listed in the library catalogues. What do you do?

You look in *The Cumulative Book Index* (if it is in the English language). For example, you have been told to read a book by David Price on the instability in the Near East, but you do not know that it is a numbered monograph in a monograph series (monograph means book), and moreover the library has not analysed this series (see the description of 'analysed series' on page 45 of this chapter). To add to your problems, you cannot find a book on that subject under the author in the library catalogue, although you know it was published in 1976. When you consult *The Cumulative Book Index* for 1977, you might come across something near your subject area under the entry 'Price, David Lynn, Oil and Middle East Security. (Georgetown Univ., Center for Strategic and Int. Studies. Washington Papers v.41 no. 43) 84p. $3. Sage Publications.' When you look in the library catalogue for 'Washington Papers,' you find the entry 'Washington Papers, no. 1– ; 1972–,' with the call number. You then request 'Washington Papers, No. 43 only.'

   You can also find the same bibliographic information in the PAIS *Bulletin* for 1977 under the subject heading 'Petroleum Industry' and the subheading 'Near East.'

---

3 Research libraries catalogue the first volume of serials they receive, and leave the entry open to indicate that succeeding volumes will be placed on the shelf after the first volume. Therefore, to find the call number, look in the library catalogue that covers the year the first volume was issued.

If the monograph were in a European language other than English, you could probably find its monograph series and its number under the same subject headings in the PAIS *Foreign Language Index.*

THE REQUEST SLIP

You know how to get to the correct department in a research library, use the reference books on the reference shelves, use the catalogues, use the periodical indexes, and request books, pamphlets, and periodicals from the stacks. All of these steps are elementary to doing research. After requesting a book from the stacks, however, instead of receiving the book, you may receive your request slip back. In this case, look at the listing of 'reports' on the slip. Some libraries list these on the reverse side of the slip, others at the bottom of the slip. In the New York Public Library, for example, the reports are listed on the reverse side, like this (see Figure 2.23):

1. 'Verify.' This means you should take your returned slip to a librarian for verification. You may have made a mistake when copying the catalogue entry. If your request was for a periodical, the librarian needs to check to see if the issue you requested is in the library. It may be in the bindery or on the current shelves.
2. 'Call no. changed' means that a publication found in the old book catalogue has been recatalogued in the computer catalogue and given a different call number.
3. 'Not on shelf' simply means that the book cannot be found on the shelf where it should be. It could be misshelved, in use (although no slip is on file for it), or lost (although not officially declared lost). You may request a 'Search and Notify,' which means the staff searches for the book and notifies you by postcard if it is located.
4. 'In use, M.R.R.' means that the book is being read at that

Fig. 2.23

Instructions to reader	For staff use
1. Consult catalogs. Print all required information on call slip. When in doubt, consult Librarian.	Verify Date? Volume?
2. If reference is to a periodical article, give title of periodical, date, and volume number.	Bound? Call no. chngd. Not on shelf In use, M.R.R.
3. Make a separate note of any information you may need later.	In use, Rm. Reserved, M.R.R.
4. Choose a seat. Copy its number on call slip and hand in slip at information desk. Material will be delivered to your seat.	Reserved, Rm. In bindery Being filmed Missing
5. If requested material or a report is not received in 20 minutes, please consult Librarian.	Not in shelf list Add'l vol's. wanted?

Filed:

moment in the Main Reading Room. 'In use, Rm–' with the room number indicated means that the book is being read in one of the departments. Try requesting the book in a few days.

5. 'Reserved' means that the book is on the reserve shelves in the Main Reading Room or in one of the departments. The name of the reader who reserved the book will be written on the back of the slip, which enables you to find the book reserved under his or her name, and take it for your use. You should return the book to the reserve shelves; otherwise it will be returned to the stacks.

6. 'In bindery' means that the book or periodical is being bound and will not be reshelved perhaps for months.

7. 'Being filmed.' If the book is actually in the process of being filmed, you cannot retrieve it. But it may be either waiting to be filmed or filmed but not catalogued, in which cases the librarian can retrieve it from the filming room for you.

8. 'Missing.' This means stolen. Look again in the catalogues to see if the book has been replaced and given a different call number, or if there are earlier or newer editions.

9. 'Not in shelf list.' The shelf list catalogue contains cards for every book and periodical title catalogued in the library. The cards are filed by call number. When the library page cannot find the book you requested, he or she checks the shelf catalogue to see if the call number is correct. If you receive the report that the book is not in the shelf list catalogue, the call number is incorrect.

10. 'Add'l vols., wanted?' means that there are many volumes per year of the series you have requested and the library page has sent up some volumes and wants to know if you want additional volumes.

11. 'On loan' means that the book you want is out on loan under the library's interlibrary loan system.

The reverse side of the slip for the library of the British Museum directs the reader to special areas where the book is shelved when it cannot be found in the stacks. (In some libraries, such as the NYPL, the librarians check request slips when you present them and direct you to the correct area before you file them).

On the request slip for the British Library reproduced in Figure 2.24 the box for checking the catalogue entry is crossed through and the words 'the entry' have been crossed out and replaced by the word 'dates.' The order is for a serial, and you are being requested to check under the main entry (where the dates of the full run of the serial is given) to make sure the library has the dates you requested. The library page can find no issue earlier than 1960.

For requesting publications at the Bibliothèque Nationale in Paris, there are two request forms or slips: one for books and the other for periodicals. The slip shown in Figure 2.25, you will notice, indicates where an error was made. In this case, the library page has returned the slip with the error circled in red pencil and a check mark in the appropriate box.

Fig. 2.24

```
REASON FOR NON-DELIVERY
─────────────────────────────────────────────────────────────────────

In use. If urgently required apply to:              This work is on the reference shelves of

  ☐  Reading Room Centre Desk              ☐  The Reading Room        ☐  The North Library
  ☐  North Library Issue Counter           ☐  The North Library Gallery  ☐  The Map Library
  ☐  Official Publications Issue Desk       ☐  The Official Publications Library
  ☐  North Library Gallery Issue Desk       ☐  Music Reading Area

Name _____ date _____          ☐  The last number of the series on the shelf at this
                                                shelf mark is _____

  ☐  At Binders       Order No _____   ☐  Please give volume number required
  ☐  At Labellers     Bindery _____               DATES
  ☐  At Furbishers    Date _____     ☒  Please check the entry in the General Catalogue
                                                 again and if necessary show the entry to the Enquiry
If urgently required apply to  The Superintendent  Book   Desk staff
Delivery Services  Reading Room
                                             ☐  This work has been transferred to the Science
It is regretted that:                            Reference Library.

  ☐  this work was destroyed by bombing in the war, we   ☐  This work is at present in the Reprographic
     have not been able to acquire a replacement            Section and is temporarily unavailable

  ☐  this work has been mislaid                   Reprographic No _____ date _____

  ☐  this work has been missing since          ☐  For Further information please apply to Book
  _____              Delivery Enquiries or Enquiry Desk

PB SDB4
                   First on shelf 1960
```

SUPPLEMENTARY CATALOGUES

Authority Catalogues

For every card in the public catalogue there is a duplicate card in the authority catalogues, which are kept in the cataloguing rooms. If you suspect a book should be in the research library but cannot find it in the public catalogue, you should ask the librarian to check the authority catalogue. Possibly the card for the item was pulled out of the old card catalogue by an irate reader (for example, cards with the subject heading 'Hitler, Adolf' were taken from the public card catalogue in NYPL and not discovered missing until years later), or a filing clerk inadvertently forgot to return a card after making corrections to it, as happened on occasion to the government publications public catalogue. The reproduction of the catalogues in book form was made from the public cata-

Fig. 2.25

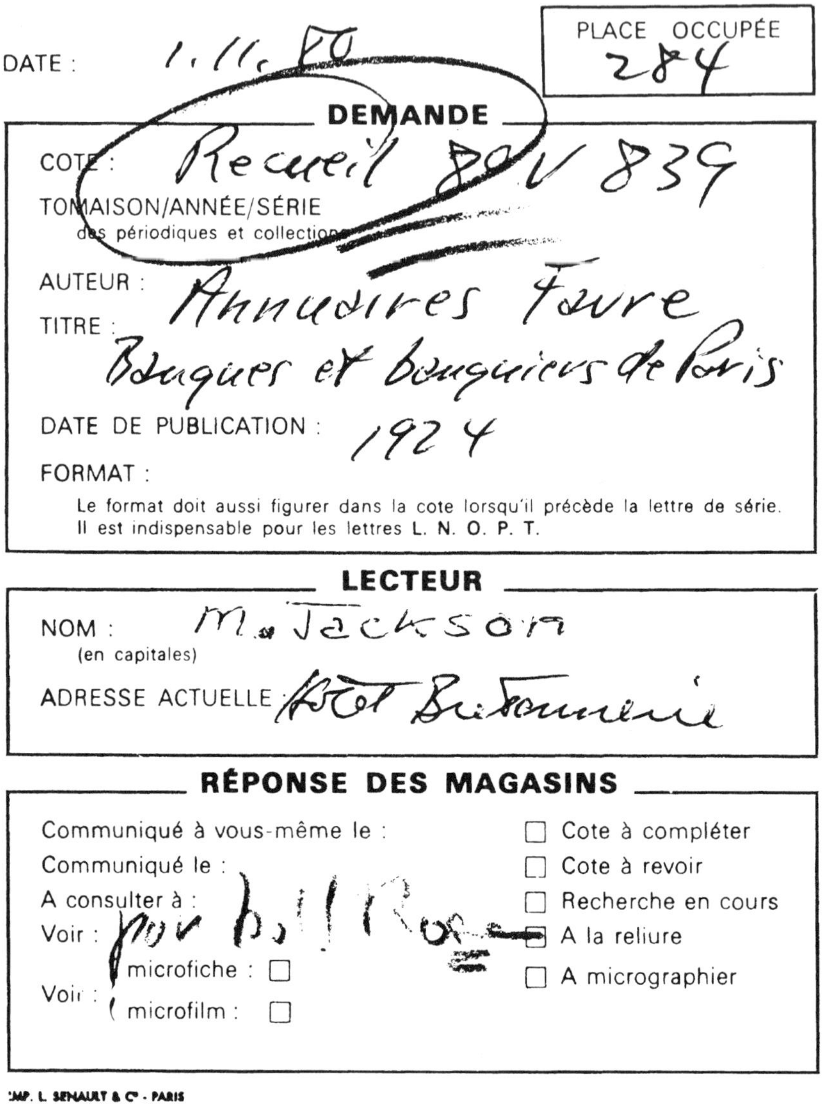

DATE : *1. 11. PO*

PLACE OCCUPÉE
284

DEMANDE

COTE : *Recueil 80 V 839*

TOMAISON/ANNÉE/SÉRIE
des périodiques et collections

AUTEUR :

TITRE : *Annuaires Faure*
Bouquers et bouquieurs de Paris

DATE DE PUBLICATION : *1924*

FORMAT :
Le format doit aussi figurer dans la cote lorsqu'il précède la lettre de série.
Il est indispensable pour les lettres L. N. O. P. T.

LECTEUR

NOM : *M. Jackson*
(en capitales)

ADRESSE ACTUELLE *Prêt Britannique*

RÉPONSE DES MAGASINS

Communiqué à vous-même le :   ☐ Cote à compléter
Communiqué le :   ☐ Cote à revoir
A consulter à : *par bil Ros*   ☐ Recherche en cours
Voir :   ☐ A la reliure
        (microfiche : ☐
Voir :   ☐ A micrographier
        (microfilm : ☐

IMP. L. SENAULT & Cⁱᵉ - PARIS

logues, not the authority catalogues; hence the book catalogues are not actually complete. With the gradual conversion of the old catalogue entries to the computer catalogue by libraries that can afford computerization, this problem should be obviated – if the conversion is being done with entries from the authority catalogues.

There are three authority catalogues: the authority name catalogue, the authority serial catalogue, and the authority government publications catalogue. The authority card establishes the correct form for that entry. In the case of Sir Winston Churchill, for instance, it refers to biographies establishing the correct form of his name, or change of name, and his birth and death dates. In the case of corporate entries, the authority card establishes the correct form for the catalogue entry, notes the background of the corporate body, its name changes, and the dates of those changes. It refers to authoritative sources for the form of entry and gives cross-references from other forms. Thus the authority catalogue is as important to a library as the birth certificate is to an individual.

With the coming of the online catalogue, much of the cataloguing of new materials became centralized, as was the case at the Library of Congress, which received the government grants to set up automated cataloguing. Hence the authority information is kept in the Cataloguing Division at the Library of Congress.

Deferred Catalogues

When books that by all reasoning should be in the research library are found neither in the public catalogue nor in the authority catalogue, ask the librarian to check the deferred catalogues. Many shelves of publications are deferred for future cataloguing. Deferred publications are often from foreign publishers and frequently are government publications. You can request a deferred publication by its deferred number. In certain years research libraries, lacking funds for cataloguing, have deferred tens of thousands of books, including new books from standard publishers. You must ask the librarian to retrieve those publications. This point cannot be emphasized enough.

Special Catalogues

Special catalogues may be in card or book form. They cover the collections in specific subject areas. Often special catalogues remain the only guide to their collections. This is generally true of manuscript collections for which the catalogue may be found only in the manuscripts room. Special collections of rare books and manuscripts such as the NYPL's Berg Collection and Arents Collections maintain catalogues peculiar to their collections alone.

In recent years many of these special supplementary catalogues have been reproduced in book form. Following is a list of such book catalogues that record the basic collections of NYPL's special or subject collections.

NYPL *Dictionary Catalog*:
   of Art and Architecture
   of the Dance Collection
   of the Henry W. and Albert A. Berg Collection of English and American Literature
   of the History of the Americas Collection
   of the Manuscript Division
   of the Map Division
   and so on.

When researching a subject that is likely to be supplemented by specialized cataloguing treatment such as music scores, photographic collections, or oral history, keep a lookout for catalogues in book form of other libraries. Here are a couple of examples:

France. Fondation Nationale des Sciences Politiques, Paris. Centre de documentation contemporaine. *Index* (Bibliographie courante d'articles des périodiques postérieurs à 1944 sur les problèmes politiques, économiques et sociales (1948) v. 1–17. From 1969 to 1978 it was updated by eleven supplements. From 1983 on, this index is found only in database form: ESOP.

Newberry Library, Chicago, Edward E. Ayer Collection. *Dictionary*

Catalog of Americana and American Indians in the Newberry Library, 16 vols. 1961. First Supp. 3 vols., 1970. Second Supp. 4 vols., 1980.

For a listing of other similar catalogues, see Bonnie R. Nelson, *A Guide to Published Library Catalogs* (Metchuen, NJ; London: Scarecrow, 1982): 'The proper use of this wide range reference book puts the world's written records into our hands.' It lists and describes major catalogues of significant collections, generally multivolume, published since 1960 (excluding the printed book catalogues of the nineteenth and early twentieth centuries). It represents entire collections from the earliest acquisitions to recent years.

Book catalogues like those issued by the British Library and the Library of the London School of Economics are printed catalogues. Printed book catalogues can cover the holdings of many libraries and are used to locate books for interlibrary loan. An example is the *National Union Catalog* (NUC), a multivolume set that lists books and pamphlets printed before 1956. The entries are by author and given the symbols for the research libraries in North America from which the book may be borrowed by your research library at your request. After 1956, decennial, quinquennial, and annual volumes follow, up to the present. Its counterpart for serials is the *Union List of Serials* and its supplements.

NYPL Catalog of Government Publications in The Research Libraries

A card catalogue reproduced in book form, the NYPL *Catalog of Government Publications in The Research Libraries* shows the library's holdings in government publications before 1972. There was a large cataloguing backlog when this catalogue was closed; therefore some government publications issued before 1972, particularly congressional hearings, are found in the NYPL Research Libraries' *Online Dictionary Catalog* (CATNYP).

The idea behind the *Government Publications* catalogue was to separate government documents from the rest of the collection in the catalogue to make them easier to find. The catalogue is arranged alphabetically by government entity of the publishing body: country, state or province, county, city or town. Within this entity, the entries are arranged alphabetically by government agency, which is listed in inverted form (e.g., Agriculture, Department of). Within the agency, government serials are arranged in alphabetical order before the monographs, which are arranged chronologically by date of publication. Because government publications are recognized most easily by government body and date of publication, you can see the value of this catalogue. It had to be abandoned when the different filing and cataloguing system of the Library of Congress became standard with the introduction of automated cataloguing.

Supplementary Catalogues

By supplementary catalogues we refer to catalogues that serve as the library catalogue because we can find the publications listed in them only in these sources, using the entry numbers in them in lieu of call numbers. Most prominent of these is the *Monthly Catalog of United States Government Publications*, which since the 1950s has provided direct access to the publications listed in it on microprint card. Since the early 1980s, when the U.S. government began publishing in microfiche, the *Monthly Catalog* has provided access, by Superintendent of Documents number, to those government publications issued in microfiche. You must use this number as a call number. Many research libraries (including the NYPL) do not enter such publications in the library catalogues. The use of the *Monthly Catalog* is described in the section on government publications in Chapter 3.

A *Checklist of Official Publications of the State of New York*, a monthly, serves the same purpose. It provides the call numbers to state publications, all of which have been reproduced in microform since 1975.

Economics Working Papers Bibliography, an annual listing of working papers in economics issued from institutions around the world, serves as the catalogue for the publications it lists, all of which are on microfiche.

Several of these kinds of catalogues exist, and you can expect more. Some have adopted the approach of the Congressional Information Service (CIS) *Index to U.S. Government Publications*, in which you find the item you wish in the detailed *Index* volume, which leads you to an abstract of the publication in the companion *Abstract* volume. Here you find a number opposite the entry that serves as a call number to the publication on microfiche located in the library's microform reading room.

Publications on Microform

Libraries recatalogue some publications listed in their retrospective catalogues because they put the publications onto microfilm or microfiche and discarded the paper volumes. The recatalogued items appear in the newer catalogues with a changed call number. In NYPL, for instance, if the publication is on microfilm, the call number begins with '*Z–.' If it was put on microfiche, the call number begins with '*X–.' When you encounter these call numbers, you proceed to the microform reading areas to read the publication.

Some departments maintain separate lists of periodicals on microfilm that were recatalogued with film call numbers.

Chapter 3

Tools of Research

No longer a novice, my dear Watson.

Feel free to skip through this section and read only what interests you. But before you plunge into the more sophisticated library tools, please be sure you are well practised in the elementaries. And always remember a basic term, *main entry*. The American Library Association (ALA) defines it as 'A full catalog entry, usually the author entry, giving all the information necessary to the complete identification of a work. In a card catalog this entry bears also the tracing of all other headings under which the work in question is entered in the catalog.'

The last sentence refers to arabic-numbered subject headings and the Roman numeral added author and title entries, as seen at the foot of the card in Figure 2.12b (p. 55). They also appear above the main entry on cards filed in the catalogue, to help you find the main entry. By using the subject tracings at the foot of a main entry card, you can find books in the catalogue under those subject headings relevant to the subject you are researching.

It is the main entry that you write opposite the author designation on your request slip, followed by the title of the book. When requesting a periodical, it is important to remember that the title is usually the main entry.

Let us suppose that the library catalogues and periodical indexes fail to lead you to the information you want. You need more sophisticated means to gain access to publications in the collection. General guides to reference works lead you to specific sources for the subject you are researching. The most widely consulted and comprehensive is Balay's *Guide to Reference Books*, 11th ed. (1996), formerly Sheehy's *Guide to Reference Books*. In the following pages you will find a few of the most-used titles as examples of standard reference works. They are briefly cited to serve as aids to your research; full bibliographic information, when needed, may be found in the general reference guides or the library catalogues.

These sources are characterized by the format by which they give you access to the collection. Each one of these formats or library tools is further characterized by the broad subject division in which it is primarily used.

THE BIBLIOGRAPHY: ITS FORMS AND USES

The ALA defines a *bibliography* as a list of books, maps, etc., differing from a catalogue in not being necessarily a list of materials in a collection, a library, or a group of libraries. The book bibliography concentrates on subjects in depth, and is sometimes an art form in itself.

You may find book bibliographies through *bibliographies of bibliographies*, which arrange bibliographies by subject, by time period, or by geographical area. For example, a list of bibliographies of the literary works of English authors of the twentieth century is a bibliography of bibliographies by subject. Here are examples found in the open reference shelves in General Research:

- *Index bibliographicus*: v.1, Science and Technology, v.2, Social Sciences; v.3, Humanities; v.4, General Bibliography.
- *A World Bibliography of Bibliographies and of Bibliographical Catalogues, Calendars, Abstracts, Digests and the Like*. 5 vols.
- *Internationale Personal Bibliographies, 1800–1987* (This indexes bibliographies contained in books, periodicals, biographical dictionaries, academic annuals, Festschriften, and other

Fig. 3.1

```
CHURCHILL, SIR WINSTON LEONARD SPENCER, 1874 – 1965
      --BIBL.                                        D – 14
                                                      9850
WOODS, FREDERICK.
    A bibliography of the works of Sir Winston Churchill.
[Toronto] University of Toronto press, 1963.    340 p.
illus., ports.   22cm.




1. Churchill, Sir Winston Leonard Spencer, 1874-  --Bibl.
NN R 3.64 e/B  OC  PC,1  SL  E,  1     (LC1,X1)
```

sources. The first edition should be consulted for many names
that were dropped from the second for political reasons.)

You may also find bibliographies by catalogue subject heading.
The letters 'BIBL.' following the subject heading indicate a bibliography (see Figure 3.1). You can see that Churchill wrote a great
deal throughout his long life because this book contains 340 pages.

Bibliographies to Books

Often bibliographies are arranged to indicate the importance of
each source and its contribution to the subject. In this vein,
descriptive and textual bibliographies place an artist's works in
chronological sequence and indicate when changes took place in
the author's viewpoint, which is helpful to a biographer.

To remain comprehensive, some book bibliographies are
updated periodically to include the latest works on the subject.
Some periodicals, for instance, devote one issue a year to listing
new publications in the subject fields they cover.

As the preceding example of the bibliography to Churchill's
works (Figure 3.1) illustrates, you can sometimes locate bibliogra-

phies to particular subjects without going through bibliographies to bibliographies. Aside from using the library catalogue, you can use bibliographies to books such as the following:

- MLA *International Bibliography of Books and Articles on the Modern Languages and Literatures*, 1921–. Annual. Since 1969 this has been divided into three sections, each with a separate table of contents, list of journal title abbreviations, and index of critics. I. General literature and English, American, Celtic, and Medieval and neo-Latin literatures, and folklore. (Australian, Canadian, Caribbean, and other English-language literatures of the world are in the opening division of the English literature section.) II. European, Asian, African, and Latin American literatures. III. General linguistics and studies of specific languages. (This reference is designed to serve the needs of those researching in a theme, idea, literary form, or similar topic.) Since 1981 two volumes were added, including one for folklore.
- *American Book Publishing Record* (a cumulation of American book production for the years 1876–1949 in 15 volumes).
- *American Book Publishing Record Cumulative*, 1950–77, in 15 volumes.
- *Index Translationum.* International bibliography of translations, 1932–. (Available on CD-ROM, 1979–).
- *Cumulative Book Index* (for publications in English), with which you are already familiar, is a bibliography to books, broadly speaking.
- *Biblio* (for publications in French) *catalogue des ouvrages parus en langue française dans le monde entier,* 1934–70 (annual); and *Les Livres de l'année, Biblio,* 1971–.
- *Deutsches Bucherverzeichnis* (for publications in German), 1915–. Continued by *Deutsche Nationalbibliographie und Bibliographie ...* Reihe E, 1986–.

Checklists

Checklist bibliographies are designed to list the works dealing with a certain subject or person, such as the following:

Gwinup, Thomas. *Greek and Roman Authors: A Checklist of Criticism,* 2nd ed. 1982.

Weixlmann, Joe. *American Short Fiction Criticism and Scholarship, 1959–1977: A Checklist,* 1982.

Kuntz, Joseph. *Poetry Explication: A Checklist of Interpretation since 1975 of British and American Poems Past and Present,* 1980.

Salem, James M. *A Guide to Critical Reviews.* I. American drama, 1909–82. II. The Musical, 1909–89. III. Foreign Drama, 1909–77.

Annotated Bibliographies

Annotated bibliographies provide description of the publications to authenticate their editions and identify them, as in the case of the anonymously published books of a forgotten author. For example:

- Morley, William F.E. *A Bibliographical Study of Major John Richardson* (Toronto: 1973).

They also help you evaluate the usefulness of a publication for your research. For example:

- Drescher, Horst. *The Contemporary English Novel: An Annotated Bibliography of Secondary Sources,* 1973.

Finally, they can provide depth of coverage. For example:

- 'Shakespeare: An Annotated Bibliography,' in *Shakespeare Quarterly* (Autumn 1950). (References are comprehensive with thorough coverage of foreign criticism. Indexes to topics, titles of plays, and characters and other proper names.)

Bibliographies of Biographies

Following are examples of bibliographies of biographies:

- Slocum, Robert. *Biographical Dictionaries and Related Works,* 1986.

(Devoted principally to biographical dictionaries representing all languages and cultures.)

- *Biography and Genealogy Master Index* (consolidated index to more than 3,200,000 biographical sketches in more than 350 current and retrospective biographical dictionaries). Supplement 1981–2 (more than 1 million additional citations to more than 140 biographical dictionaries). Cumulated at five-year intervals.

Bibliographies of Monographic Series

You will recall that you can discover the titles of monographic series by author, title, and subject of publications in English through the *Cumulative Book Index*. There is, however, a comprehensive bibliography devoted to monographic series: *Monographic series*, v. 1– , 1976–. This is a compilation of Library of Congress printed card catalogues representing all monographs catalogued by the library. By identifying the individual monographs issued in a series, this catalogue serves both as a reference tool and as an acquisitions aid. Popular as well as scholarly series issued anywhere in the world are represented.

Bibliographies of Directories

An example of this type of bibliography is *Canadian Directories, 1790–1987: a bibliography and place-name index* (Ottawa: National Library of Canada, 1989) 3 v. (a directory of 1,200 directories arranged chronologically, then by province, city, town, township, county, district or region).

Periodical Indexes

Periodical indexes are guides to articles in magazines and newspapers. To determine which periodical indexing service indexes the periodical in which you are interested, look in *Ulrich's International Directory to Periodicals*, which gives the indexing source (if there is one) following the description of publisher, frequency, and price of the periodical. *Ulrich's* also notes that the periodical is available on CD-ROM and online. Please note that some electronic resources are free while others are very expensive and will not be available in libraries that cannot afford to subscribe to them.

Periodical indexes cover specific subject fields, which are evident by their titles. Following are listings, under the appropriate divisions usually found in libraries, of some of the periodical indexes you can find on the reference shelves. The latter years of the ongoing periodicals can also be found on CD-ROM or the Internet, provided the library subscribes to these services.

General Research or Humanities Division

Poole's Index to Periodical Literature, 1802–1907
Nineteenth Century Reader's Guide, 1900–22
Reader's Guide to Periodical Literature, 1905–
International Index to Periodicals, 1907–65:
  Social Sciences and Humanities Index, 1965–74
  Humanities Index, 1974–
  Social Sciences Index, 1974–
Bibliographie der deutschen Zeitschriftenliteratur, 1896–1964
Bibliographie der fremdsprachigen Zeitschriftenliteratur/Répertoire bibliographique international des revues/International Index to Periodicals, 1911–64
Internationale Bibliographie der Zeitschriftenliteratur aus allen Gebieten des Wissens, 1963/4–
Education Index, 1929–
Index to Legal Periodicals, 1908–
Index to Foreign Legal Periodicals, 1960–
Index to Religious Periodical Literature, 1949–75/76
  Religion Index One, 1977–
Biography Index, 1947–
French Periodical Index, 1973/74–

Notable Electronic Resources:

American Book Prices Current
Anthropological Literature

Archives USA
ATLA Religion Index
British Humanities Index
Contemporary Women's Issues
FRANCIS
Hispanic American Periodicals Index
Humanities Index
Literature Online
MLA International Bibliography
Psyclit
Sociofile

Economic Social and Business Affairs Division

Business Periodicals Index, 1958– (formerly the *Industrial Arts Index,*
    1913–57).
Public Affairs Information Service, *Bulletin,* 1915–
Funk and Scott Index to Corporations, 1960–
    F & S Index, Europe, 1978–
    F & S Index, International, 1968–
    F & S Index of Corporate Change, 1978–
Combined Retrospective Index to Journals in Political Science, 1886–1974.
United States Political Science Documents, 1975–
U.S. Government Periodicals Index, 1994–

CD-ROMs:

Business Abstracts: an online index of business periodicals with
    abstracts
Compustat: a CD-ROM directory with historical financial informa-
    tion on Canadian and U.S. companies
EconLit: an online index of economic literature with abstracts
Worldscope: a CD-ROM directory providing corporate profiles and
    financial information on companies worldwide

Internet:

ABI/Inform: Index to over 800 business periodicals with full text

CBCA (*Canadian Business and Current Affairs*): Full text to articles in 200 Canadian business periodicals, nearly 300 popular magazines, and 10 newspapers.

Science and Technology Division

Applied Science and Technology Index, 1958–
Agricultural Index, 1919–64
Biological and Agricultural Index, 1964–
Index Medicus, 1960–

Notable Electronic Resources:

Argus Clearing House: a guide to evaluated Web resources in architecture, construction, industrial engineering, and transportation. There are other guides for the Earth Sciences, Physics, Chemistry, Botany, as well as for Arts and Humanities, Business and Employment, Government and Law, Health and Medicine, Environment, Social Sciences, etc., found on the Web at http://www.clearinghouse.net/ – for example, *Ei Compendex* (Engineering Index on the Web).

Engineering E-journal Search Engine (full text of 100 engineering e-journals)

Agricola: National Agricultrual Library searchable database of bibliographical information about all aspects of agriculture and allied disciplines: a books database and an articles database

Journal of High Energy Physics: a full-text journal

Health Sciences on the Web: British Medical Journal; Canadian Medical Association Journal; Journal of the American Medical Association; New England Journal of Medicine; Pediatrics

Genealogy Division

Genealogical Periodical Index, 1962–
American Genealogical-Biographical Index, 1952–93

Internet:

Ancestry.com (http://www.ancestry.com)

Art and Architecture Collection

Art Index, 1929–
Art bibliographies Modern

Slavonic Division

American Bibliography of Slavic and East European Studies, 1967–
Letopis zhurnal 'nykh statei, 1926–

Oriental Division

Guide to Indian Periodical Literature, 1964–
Fihrist (Arabic)
Turkiye makaleler bibliografyasi (Turkey), 1952–
Zasshi Kiji sakuin (Japan), 1948–

Music Division

Music Index, 1949–
Musical Article Guide, 1966–

Theatre Collection

Dramatic Index, 1909–49
Guide to the Performing Arts, 1957–68
Guide to the Musical Arts, 1953–6
International Index to Film Periodicals, 1972–

Dance Collection

Guide to Dance Periodicals, 1931/5–1961/2
Index to Dance Periodicals, 1990–

Schomburg Center

> *Index to Black Periodicals,* 1984–
> *Index to Periodicals by and about Negroes,* 1960–70
> *Kaiser Index to Black Resources,* 1948–85

Indexes to Newspapers

Online indexes to newspapers have increased dramatically in recent years. Coverage, especially full text, is often limited to 1997 on, but there are exceptions noted below.

> *Index to the Times* (London)
> *Index to the New York Times*
> *Index to the Wall Street Journal*
> *Al-Ahram Index* (Cairo)
> *Letopis gazetnykh statei* (for Russia. There are also separate indexes for each Soviet republic).

Newspapers are sometimes indexed in periodical indexes – for example, the *Funk and Scott Index* includes the *Wall Street Journal* and the *New York Times.* The *Federal Index* includes the *Washington Post.*

Newspapers are indexed in data banks: the *Globe and Mail* (Toronto) and the *New York Times* have individual databases back to the 1970s. Every large research library will have newspaper indexes on CD-ROM and/or on the Internet. For example, Chadwyck-Healey, a private corporation specializing in making archives available on microfiche, has made available *Palmer's Index to the Times* [of London], *1709–1905,* the *Official Index to the Times, 1905–1980,* and the *Historical Index to the New York Times, 1851– 1920,* on both CD-ROM and the World Wide Web. *Global Newsbank, Canadian News Disc, Canadian Business and Current Affairs, CEDI-ROM,* UMI's *Proquest Direct Newspaper,* all index and, in some cases, provide full text of U.S., UK, and Canadian newspapers online.

Some bibliographies list indexes to newspapers held by a particular library or region. You can find references to them on the Internet or on one of the library online networks and order them through interlibrary loan. The periods and publications covered by indexes can vary greatly; for instance, on the open shelves of the Newspaper Division of the British Library may be found 66 indexes such as *A Local Index to the Dumfries and Galloway Standard Advertiser and its Predecessors over 200 Years, 1777–1925; Index to Selected Articles published in the Jewish Chronicle, 1841–1933; The Spiritualist Index, 1869–1882; Couriere della Serra Index, 1914–77; Messager de Tahiti Index, 1852–83; Tables du Journal de Temps, 1861–1900;* and the *Clover Newspaper Index* (covering the *Daily Telegraph,* the *Financial Times,* the *Guardian,* the *Observer,* and the *Sunday Times*), September 1986– , and so on.

For further information, see Anita Cheek Milner, *Newspaper Indexes: A Location and Subject Guide for Researchers,* 1977–83; and John Pluce, *Newspaper Indexes in the Newspaper and Current Periodical Room* (Library of Congress), 1987.

Indexes to Literature Reviews

Some indexes are used primarily for reviewing current literature.

General Research and Humanities Division

> *Book Review Digest,* 1905– , gives brief quotations from reviews of published books and citations to other reviews.
> Periodicals such as *Publishers' Weekly, Choice, Library Journal,* and the *Reprint Bulletin* review recent publications.

Economic Social and Business Affairs Division

> *Journal of Economic Literature,* issued monthly by the American Economic Association, carries book reviews and abstracts of articles and books.
> *Index of Economic Articles* indexes articles and books by subject classification number.

Sciences and Technology

New Technical Books, 1915–

Indexes That Give Abstracts

Abstracts of articles, books, and research papers may consist of a few lines or a long paragraph. With the abstract you will find the title, date, volume, and page numbers of the publication where the full article or report can be found.

General Research and Humanities Division

> *Historical Abstracts*: Bibliography of the World's Historical Litera-
> ture, issued quarterly beginning in 1955, with an annual index
> covering more than 30 languages and 85 countries, excluding
> the United States and Canada. Part A: Modern History Abstracts,
> 1450–1914. Part B: Twentieth Century Abstracts, 1914.
> For the United States and Canada use *America. History and Life,*
> 1964–. Part A: Article Abstracts and Citations; Part B: Index to
> Book Reviews; Part C: American History Bibliography (of articles
> cited in Part A, new books cited in Part B, and dissertations);
> Annual; Part D: Annual Index (cumulative subject indexes to
> Parts A, B, C, book review index, book title index, list of abstract-
> ers, and list of periodicals).
> *Psychological Abstracts,* 1927
> *Resources in Education,* a monthly abstract 'permitting the early
> identification and acquisition of reports.'
> *Dissertations Abstracts International* abstracts MA theses and PhD dis-
> sertations from universities around the world and provides a
> number by which you can order the work in photocopy or micro-
> form from a central clearinghouse. This appears monthly in two
> series: humanities and social science series and science series. It
> relates the latest university research. Most libraries no longer
> acquire dissertations. You may call up *Dissertations Abstracts* on
> the Internet on a search engine and find a few listings, from *Pro-*

Quest and *FirstSearch*, but they require a subscription to access them. Libraries provide free access.

Economic Social and Business Affairs Division

Sociological Abstracts, 1952–
Work Related Abstracts, 1973–
   Employment Relations Abstracts, 1959–72
   Labor Personnel Index, 1950–8
American Statistics Abstracts, 1973–. You must use its companion volume *The American Statistics Index* to find the abstracts in the *Abstracts* volume. (The Congressional Information Service's *Abstracts to U.S. Government Publications* is a similar publication. See the section on Government Publications.)

Indexes to Special Issues of Periodicals

Another form of index that is used as a guide more to current than to past literature is an index that indicates which issues of which periodicals contain special information, such as listings of trade shows, buyers, or dealers – for example, the *Guide to Special Issues and Indexes of Periodicals*. Although issued only every few years, it is valuable for current material because it indicates, for example, that the May 15 issue of *Fortune* magazine lists the top 500 corporations, so that you can seek that issue for the current year to find the latest listing.

Consumers Index (to product evaluations and information sources) provides monthly brief annotations about the articles cited.

Bibliographical Lists, Citation Indexes, Reports

An example of this rarer type of index is *Exchange Bibliographies*, issued by the Committee of Industrial Relations Librarians. It is valuable for the variety and individuality of its approach to subject themes.

Citation Indexes

If you wish to find articles that have referred to a certain author and his or her article, the following periodical citation indexes can be used:

Arts and Humanities Citation Index, 1976–
Social Sciences Citation Index, 1972–
Sciences Citation Index, 1961–

Guides to Reports, Research Papers, Conference Proceedings

Institutions often issue indexes to their publications, such as the Conference Board's *Cumulative Index* (in Economic and Public Affairs) and the Rand Institute's *Index* to its reports (in Science and Technology).

The annual *Economic Working Papers Bibliography* lists research papers issued by university research centres and institutes. Research libraries acquire these working papers not in book form, but in microfiche; the *Bibliography* provides the numbers by which they are filed (in Economic and Public Affairs).

Some of the indexes for conference proceedings found in the General Research Division are as follows:

- *Index to Social Sciences and Humanities Proceedings,* issued quarterly with annual cumulations with author, editor, corporate, and permutation indexes to its main section listing the contents of the published proceedings.
- *Directory of Published Proceedings* guides you to preprints and published proceedings of congresses, conferences, symposia, meetings, seminars, and summer schools held worldwide from 1964 to date, with a location index and subject/sponsor index. These proceedings will be found under the name of the sponsoring organization in the library catalogue. For the most part they are catalogued as individual monographs. Sometimes, however, they are treated as a series, in which case you must locate the entry for the first conference in the library catalogue

and indicate on your request slip the number or date of the conference you want.

• *World Meetings: Social and Behavioral Sciences, Human Services and Management*: a two-year registry of future meetings (quarterly). For future medical, scientific, and technical meetings use

World Meetings: United States and Canada
World Meetings: Outside the United States and Canada
World Meetings: Medicine

Primary Information and Current Facts

While most of the foregoing bibliographies and indexes include citations to sources you must find somewhere in the library, and hence are indexes to secondary sources, some indexes lead you directly to the information in the same volume or the same series of volumes. *Facts on File, Keesing's Contemporary Archives*, and the *African Economic and Political Research Index* provide quick reference to news events because the information is given in the same volume as the index.

Similarly, the many annual almanacs such as the *Information Please Almanac, World Almanac*, and *Whittaker's* (for Great Britain) are indexes to facts and addresses. The *World of Learning* lists all institutions (e.g., museums, art galleries, universities, etc.) by country. The *Statesman's Yearbook* includes an index at the back of the volume to the geographic, demographic, social, and economic facts about nations in the remainder of the volume. The *Europa Yearbook* provides the same sort of annual guide to primary information about the world's nations, their institutions, leaders, and statistics.

Many governments issue statistical yearbooks in this category, such as *Statistical Yearbook of the United States, Japan Statistical Yearbook, United Nations Statistical Yearbook*, and *New York State Statistical Yearbook*.

Of course, encyclopedias like the *Britannica* are primary source indexes, as are the many biographical dictionaries: *Grove's Dictionary to Musicians*, the *Dictionary of National Biography, Current Biog-*

raphy (which contains an index to the biographical articles in earlier volumes), and the *Marquis Who's Who Publications Index* (1974–84), which lists alphabetically the names of biographies and page numbers to their biographical information in 14 current *Marquis Who's Who* biographical directories (continued by *Marquis Who's Who Index to Who's Who Books*, 1985–).

A final example of a primary-source index is *Art Prices Current*, a record of sales prices at the principal London, continental, and American auction rooms, 1908–. (It also indexes artists, engravers, and collectors.)

Current Material

Because periodical indexes appear several weeks after the issues of the periodicals they index, for very recent articles you have to look over the list of contents of the current issues of periodicals, which you can get at the library's current periodical desk. To find which periodicals are in your field, use *Ulrich's International Periodicals Directory, Standard Periodicals Directory* (for the United States), *Gale Directory of Publications* (for newspapers), *Black List: Guide to Publications in the Black World, National Directory of Newsletters and Reporting Services, Directory of Business and Financial Services*, or *Bacon's Publicity Checker.*

Some reference works provide information on current activities. For example, the *Publishers' Trade List Annual* lists books currently published, by publisher, and is used by authors hoping to sell manuscripts. The *Literary Market Place* gives authors the names of editors to whom they can send manuscripts.

Financial investors depend on Standard and Poor's *Corporation Records* for current data on businesses and S&P's *Stock Guides* and *Bond Guides* for current prices. The *Value Line* analyses firms on the stock markets on a current basis.

Some periodicals are devoted to bringing you current articles in translation, such as *Eastern European Economics*, which translates into English. For papers translated into English on various subjects, look for U.S. Joint Publications Research Service (JPRS) *Monographs*, currently announced in *U.S. Government Research and*

Development Reports (semimonthly) and listed in the *Monthly Catalog of U.S. Government Publications.*

Some libraries maintain current vertical files of clippings from newspapers, magazines, and pamphlets organized under subject headings, although with the prevalence of search engines and other online indexes permitting keyword and natural-language searching, this labour-intensive activity has become less common.

Special Lists

Some lists are invaluable to the researcher trying to trace back businesses or organizations through their former names. *The Cumulative Book Index* lists publishers and traces back their forbears, which is useful if you are searching for the owner of a copyright on a book or tracing the origins of publications and typesetting plates. *The Banker's Almanac and Yearbook* (West Sussex, England: Reed, 1919/20 –) for the United Kingdom lists banks and their predecessors, tracing amalgamations and so on, which is useful for locating archival papers. Knowlegeable librarians can inform you where to find such lists.

Special Materials

Microform

- U.S. Library of Congress, *National Register of Microform Masters*, a catalogue of master microforms that have been produced for the sole purpose of preserving printed material on film (for making other copies), reports master microforms on foreign and domestic books, pamphlets, serials, and foreign doctoral dissertations, but excludes technical reports, typescript translations, foreign or domestic archival manuscript collectibles, U.S. doctoral dissertations, and master's theses.
- *Guide to Microforms in Print*, 1978–. Incorporates *International Microforms in Print.*
- U.S. Library of Congress, *Newspapers in Microform: Foreign Countries*, 1948–83. (The dates given refer to dates of reporting not

to dates of original publications. A geographical arrangement of more than 8000 newspaper titles, from all periods, as reported by 258 U.S. and 266 foreign libraries, as well as many commercial firms. All reported locations are given.)

- U.S. Library of Congress, *Newspapers in Microform: United States,* 1948–83. (Again, the dates refer to when the libraries reported holdings to the Library of Congress.)
- New York State Library, *Checklist of Newspapers in Microform in the New York State Library* (1979).
- A *Union List of Selected Microform in Libraries in the New York Metropolitan Area* (1979).

Manuscripts

Two forms of guides to manuscript collections exist: (1) those that list the actual manuscripts and their locations, and (2) those that list archives and give some idea of the range of subjects of manuscripts found there.

Manuscript Lists:

- U.S. Library of Congress, *National Union Catalog of Manuscript Collections,* issued periodically from 1959, gives the location and number of items, and also reports archival materials and manuscript collections in microform.
- Hamer's Guide to Archives and Manuscripts in the United States
- U.S. National Archives, *Guide*
- Great Britain, Public Record Office, *Guide.* For full summaries of records transmitted to the Public Record Office, see *Reports of the Deputy Keeper of the Records.*
- Great Britain, Historical Manuscripts Commission. *Reports* are indexed in its *A Guide to the Reports on Collections of Manuscripts of Private Families, Corporations and Institutions in Great Britain and Ireland*: Pt. I, 'topographical' (cd. 7594), 1914; Pt. II, 'Index of Persons, 1870–1911,' 1935, 1938; 'Index of Persons, 1911–1957,' 1966.

- Great Britain, Historical Manuscripts Commission, *Bulletin of the National Register of Archives*, no. 1– , 1947–.

Since 1923 the Institute of Historical Research, London University, published in its *Bulletin* lists of migrations of historical manuscripts in two parts: Part I: Information from booksellers and auctioneers' catalogues about manuscripts, offered for sale; Part II: annual reports from national and local repositories on manuscripts received by them. Pressure on the *Bulletin* necessitated that Part II be taken over by the Historical Manuscript Commission's *Bulletin of the National Register of Archives* in 1955. There is an *Index to Lists of Accessions to Repositories*, 1954–8. From 1959, *Lists of Accessions* has been printed as a separate publication of the Commission. Summaries of all reports received were printed in the Commission's *Annual Reports*. The Historical Manuscripts Research Centre, Quality Lane, London, provides an immensely valuable service in locating manuscripts for researchers. Also, the Business Archives Council in London coordinates the collection of papers of firms, banks, institutions, and so on, with affiliated councils in other European countries and provides a fine reference service.

In other European countries institutions individually print catalogues of their manuscript holdings, which you may find in a research library's catalogues either by subject heading or by the institution as corporate-author main entry. These countries do not have a national coordinating body that lists manuscript accessions. The individual publications, however, are listed in the national bibliographies, which you must search through to be sure of finding.

Manuscript Archive Lists:

- *Location Register* (of twentieth-century English-language manuscripts and letters), 2 vols (London: British Library, 1988).
- Bond's *Guide to the Records of the British Houses of Parliament* (London: HMSO, 1971).
- P.K. Grimstead, *Archives and Manuscript Repositories in the USSR:*

Moscow and Leningrad, serves 'as a starting point for the foreigner planning research in the Soviet Union,' 1972.

Numerous guides like these are found in the catalogues of large research libraries.

Films

- U.S. Library of Congress, *Author Catalog,* a cumulative list of works represented by Library of Congress printed cards, 1948–52: for motion pictures and film strips.
  1953–7, L.C. National Union Catalog, v. 28
  1958–62 the same, vols. 53 and 54
  1963–7, 2 separate vols. in the N.U.C. set
  1968–72, 4 separate volumes in the N.U.C. set
  1973–7, 7 vols. in the N.U.C. set
- *Films and Other Materials for Projection,* 1978
- *Audiovisual Materials,* 1980–

Photographic and Print Collections

As part of the New York Public Library's Wallach Division of Art, Prints, and Photographs Division, the Photographic Collection maintains a card catalogue near the Print Collection card catalogue in Room 308.

Actual photographs kept in Collections are distinguished from photographs in books. There are several thousand collections of actual photographs in NYPL from the many divisions that have been brought together in a single location. (A collection can have from one to thousands of images. For instance, the Robert Dennis Stereograph [double image] Collection in the New York Public Library has 70,000 images and is international in scope.) The collections have been catalogued separately by photographer, type of issue (format, portfolio, etc.), and added entries (which can amount to as many as 20 subject entries). They are found in a unique catalogue.

Photographs in books, however, are found in the general

library catalogue under the author and the subject of the book. The parts of the collection acquired before 1952 and after 1982 may be located in the collection's shelf list catalogue by the call number 'MF.' The collection acquired between 1952 and 1982, however, was assigned fixed location call numbers, which means they are not together in the shelf list and are therefore not as easy to locate.

Other research libraries maintain different arrangements, about which you should enquire in the division that holds the photographic collections – for instance, the Sayre photo collection of actors in the University of Washington Libraries (Seattle, Washington).

Records and Tapes

Libraries have their own unique way of cataloguing and accessing the records and tapes in their collections. For instance, the Rodgers and Hammerstein Archives of Recorded Sound in the Performing Arts Research Center at Lincoln Center represents more than a half-million records, tapes, and other forms, 80 percent of which are uncatalogued. The items are filed by the name of the record company and the number it gave them. They are located through record company catalogues and national record catalogues – for instance, *Schwann Record and Tape Guide* (1949–71); *Schwann-1, Records and Tapes* (1972–Nov. 1983); *Schwann-2* (semi-annual supp.); *The New Schwann* (Dec. 1983–). In a cooperative venture with the Recorded Sound Index Company, the Archives have been entering accessions onto the RLIN online in recent years. Audio-visual and audio cassette titles are listed with their publishers in the *Video Source Book* (National Video Clearing House), 1979– , and *Words on Cassette* (New Providence, NJ: Bowker), 1992– , which merged *Words on Tape* (1984/5–1991) with *On Cassette* (1985–).

The Archives has the Rigler Deutsch Index, a microfiche index of label information transcribed from approximately 500,000 78-rpm discs held by the five major American sound archives – the other four being the Library of Congress and Yale, Stanford, and

Syracuse universities. Among the unique, noncommerical materials held by the Archives is a collection of 10,000 broadcast tapes featuring local historical and political events from 1938 to 1970 from the New York municipal radio station WNYC.

Government Publications

Government publications offer a wealth of information on just about every conceivable subject and are indispensable to economic planners and research consultants to governments and private industry. Researchers in the social sciences also find them useful. The problem is how to locate them.

First, you should know that many public research libraries put government publications with the rest of the collection, but they keep guides to these publications and to government archives in special areas. Most university libraries and other research libraries such as the British Library, on the other hand, have separate departments for government publications. In the NYPL Research Libraries, for instance, both guides and government publications are in the Science, Industry and Business Library (SIBL).

Second, governments designate certain libraries as depositories for their 'depository' publications, which are free of charge to those libraries. The U.S. government identifies depository publications in the following way:

> Depository libraries are permitted to receive one copy of all publications of the U.S. government except those determined by their issuing components to be required for official use only or those required for strictly administrative or operational purposes which have no public interest or educational value, and publications classified for reasons of national security. In addition to the exceptions noted, the so-called cooperative publications, which must necessarily be sold in order to be self-sustaining, are also excluded.

Depository libraries are designated by U.S. Code Title 44 Chap. 19. They include two libraries for each congressional district, two libraries to be designated by each senator in every state, the libraries of land-grant colleges, libraries of independent agencies of government, and libraries of executive departments.

Actually, most depository libraries select from among U.S. publications marked for deposit. In New York State, for example, only the State Library in Albany accepts all U.S. government depository publications. As for the U.S. nondepository government publications, because they must be purchased, few libraries have them. Fortunately, research libraries subscribe to the Readex Microprint Service, which provides the full texts of all depository and nondepository publications appearing in the *Monthly Catalog of U.S. Publications* (from 1955 and 1953, respectively) on microprint cards kept in the libraries. By indicating the date of the catalogue, the serial number of an item, and whether the item is depository or nondepository, you can get direct access to it.[1]

The New York Public Library's policy on government depository material is as follows: United States (select depository); Canada (depository for serials and statistics publications); Australia, Netherlands, Sweden (automatic receipt of publications from statistical agencies); United Nations (depository for items from New York); UNESCO (depository for publications from Paris); International Labor Organization (comprehensive subscription); Organization for Economic Cooperation and Development (depository); Organization of American States (comprehensive subscription); state governments – California, New Jersey, New York, Washington (depository); New York City (depository).

Third, you should approach government monographs by the year of publication; you can approach government serials as you do other serials, by title or corporate entry.[2]

Fourth, think of government publications in *geographic terms.* Approach them by country of publication. Within that country, approach them by governmental level – national, state, county, or

---

1 In the *Monthly Catalog* a black dot (i.e., '• item') after the bibliographic description indicates a depository item; no black dot indicates a nondepository item. Look up a depository item in the library catalogue first, to see if the library has it in paper.
2 The volumes of the NYPL's *Catalog of Government Publications in The Research Libraries* exemplify these approaches by the manner in which the entries are organized.

municipal government. Take the United States as an example: you are confronted with three main indexes corresponding to three levels of government:

1. On the federal level: the *Monthly Catalog of United States Government Publications* (Washington, DC: Government Printing Office)
2. On the state level: the *Monthly Checklist of State Publications* (Washington, DC: Library of Congress)
3. On the local level: the *Index to Current Urban Documents* (Westport, CT: Greenwood Press) (http://www.urbdocs.com)

At the local level of government (county and municipal publications), the *Index to Current Urban Documents* is issued quarterly, cumulated annually, and arranged geographically with a subject index. If the publications in microfiche are not held by the research library you are using, you may obtain them on microfiche from the publisher of the *Index*. It also gives the Web site address for the government departments issuing the publications. Beginning with Volume 29 in August 2000, the *Index* eliminated the microfiche in favour of offering the documents online; it is retaining the cumulative print edition.

At the state government level, you find the *Monthly Checklist of State Publications* cumulated with a subject index annually since 1910. This is a selective checklist; for a complete checklist you must consult the guides published by each state. For example, New York State issues the *Checklist of Official Publications of the State of New York* (1947–).

For the historical researcher in state publications (*Index of Economic Material in Documents of the States*),[3] Adelaide Hasse indexed the documents of some states by issuing agency and subject, and listed the titles of legislative documents with their numbers.

On the national level, the profusion of government publica-

---

3 This indexes material from the following states, from their date of establishment to 1904: California, Delaware, Illinois, Massachusetts, Kentucky, Maine, New Hampshire, New Jersey, New York, Ohio, Pennsylvania, Rhode Island, Vermont.

tions is so great that there are numerous guides to them. We will take these guides in order of relevance to the average researcher:

1. *Monthly Catalog of U.S. Government Publications.* This is the most complete guide to the publications issued since 1885, although at one time it was said to have missed 40 percent of what was being published. The bibliographic citations to publications appear in the *Monthly Catalog,* about four months after the items are published. Therefore, if a publication was printed late in 1980, you would expect to find it listed in the catalogue for 1981.

   The monthly issues have subject, title, and author indexes, which are cumulated annually. Bibliographical citations to government serials in the *Monthly Catalog* are printed in a separate annual volume. Before June 1976 they were listed in the February issue of each year.

   You should know of the *Cumulative Index,* by subject to the *Monthly Catalogs* from 1900 to 1971 – a blessed time-saver for historical researchers.

2. United States, Superintendent of Documents, *Documents Catalogs,* was published annually from 1893 to 1940 and arranged by issuing agency and subject. These volumes give better coverage than the *Monthly Catalogs* for those years.

3. *Ames Index, 1881–1893,* provides a subject guide to U.S. government publications for this period.

4. Poore's *A Descriptive Catalog of the Government Publications of the United States, 1774–1881,* is commonly known as 'Poore's.' Ben Perley Poore described as many publications as he could find, arranged them chronologically by year of issue, and provided a subject index.

   In these guides, you can find congressional committees for hearings, committee reports, and committee prints. You then find the hearings and committee prints by committee in the library catalogues. Congressional reports, however, require an intermediary step: after you have found their report numbers in one of the guides, you must consult the *Numerical Lists* for their volume number in the congressional serial set.

5. *Numerical Lists* are arranged by Congress and Session and then by Senate Documents, House Documents, Senate Reports, and House Reports. Opposite each entry is the volume number of the congressional serial set. Congressional Committee reports are bound in the serial set, the volumes of which are numbered consecutively beginning with the Fifteenth Congress. Reports for the first 14 Congresses are bound in numbered volumes called the American State Papers. To request Senate Report 347 of the 72nd Congress, 1st session, for example, you would write down the serial set volume number, that is, 9487 (which you find in the *Numerical Lists*), and the call number for the serial set (which you find in the library catalogue). You will find Senate Report 347 bound in numerical order with other Senate Reports. The Congressional Information Service has published the U.S. *Serial Set Index* (a duplication of the *Numerical Lists* with subject indexes) to facilitate research.

6. Indexes to Congressional Hearings were issued in volumes, each spanning several years, with the first covering hearings before 1935. They are arranged by committee and then by subject. If you need the subcommittee name as well, however, use the *Monthly Catalog*.

   In some libraries you may have difficulty locating the call number for U.S. congressional hearings. This is because the catalogue format was changed about 1972 from a library's particular method to the standard method set by the U.S. Library of Congress to conform to the centralized automated cataloguing, and because hearings have been published on microfiche since the late 1970s.

   In the New York Public Library, for example, you look for congressional hearings held before 1965 in the *NYPL Catalog of Government Publications in The Research Libraries* under United States, the name of the main committee (which will be in inverted form for purposes of filing alphabetically) and the Congress and Session [for example: United States. Judiciary Committee (Senate 42:2)]. (See Figure 3.2.)

   There was a large backlog of government publications waiting to be catalogued in the 1960s, hence many hearings from

Fig. 3.2 From the *Monthly Catalog of United States Government Publications* for February 1963, you find that the Senate Judiciary Committee published hearings on the constitutional rights of American Indians (serial entry no. 2098). You then find both first and second parts in the *NYPL Catalog of Government Publications in The Research Libraries* under Committee and number of Congress. The call number is 'HBC.' Let us take the entry above it (2097) on concentration ratios as a nondepository committee print. You will find it in the *Catalog of Government Publications* under the entry 'United States. Census Bureau.' This is the main entry. But fortunately it is also catalogued under its added entry, 'United States. Judiciary Committee,' by which you locate it. If the library had not acquired this committee print, you could read it on microprint card by citing 'Feb. 1963, 2097, nondepository' as a form of call number.

Serial
entry
number

Superintendent ¡ of Documents
classification number

FEBRUARY 1963

Judiciary Committee, Senate

2097   Concentration ratios in manufacturing industry, 1958, report prepared by
Bureau of Census for Subcommittee on Antitrust and Monopoly, pt. 2.
iv + 453–510 p. (Committee print, 87th Congress, 2d session.) *Paper,
25c.
L.C. card 62–61726   Y 4.J 89/2:M 31/pt.2

Constitutional rights of American Indian, hearings before Subcommittee
on Constitutional Rights, 87th Congress, 1st session pursuant to S. Res.
53. • Item 1042
L.C. card 63–606237   Y 4.J 89/2:In 2/5/pt.1◄┘
2098   pt.1. Aug. 29–Sept. 1, 1961. 1962. v + 1–284 + xxxi p. il. map.

HBC

UNITED STATES. Judiciary committee (Senate, 87:1)
    Constitutional rights of the American Indian.
Hearings before the Subcommittee on constitutional
rights of the Committee on the judiciary, United
States Senate. Eighty-seventh Congress, first session,
pursuant to S.Res. 53.   Washington, U.S. Govt.
print. off., 1962.   2 v.   fold.map   23 cm.

    Hearing held Aug. 29–Sept. 1, Nov. 25, 29, and–Dec. 2, 1961.
1. Indians, N.A. – Government relations.
NN 3.63f/j OD ED PC.1 SL AH.1 (LC1, X1)

United States.Judiciary committee (Senate, 87:2)
                                    SDG
UNITED STATES. Census bureau.
    Concentration ratios in manufacturing industry
1958. Report prepared for the Subcommittee on
antitrust and monopoly of the Committee on the judiciary,
United States Senate. Together with individual
views. Washington, U.S. Govt. print. off., 1962.
2 pts. in 1 v. (xi,510 p.)   24cm.

    "87th Congress, 2d session. Committee print."

1. Industries – Stat. – U.S. I. United States. Judiciary committee
    (Senate, 87:2) t. 1962.
NN S 12.65 1/J ODt, I Edt, PC.1, I SL (E)1 (LC1,X1,Z3)

that period were catalogued with hearings from the 1970s in the online catalogue. Thus you must check both catalogues to find some hearings and committee prints.

From 1978 through 1980, NYPL purchased hearings on microfiche from the Congressional Information Service (CIS) and discarded the paper copies. Therefore, you must locate hearings from the 95th Congress, 2nd Session, and the 96th Congress in the CIS Abstracts volumes, which give you the number for locating the microfiche in the library. Since 1978 the library has not catalogued U.S. congressional hearings.

After 1980 (the 97th Congress and successive Congresses), the U.S. government published congressional hearings on microfiche, and NYPL accepted hearings on microfiche from the government instead of purchasing them from CIS. Therefore, to locate congressional hearings held from 1980 on, you look them up in the *Monthly Catalog* to find their Superintendent of Documents' numbers by which their microfiche is located in the library. These hearings are also not catalogued in the NYPL catalogues.[4]

7. *Committee prints* are looked up in the *Monthly Catalog*. The catalogue gives you the Committee and Subcommittee that issued them, which you use to find them in the library catalogues.

8. The *Congressional Record* contains the debates in Congress, with an index volume to each congressional session. Here you find synopses of bills and can follow their progress through committees into law and find report numbers dealing with these bills. The Commerce Clearing House (CCH) issues a looseleaf service, the *Congressional Index*, which helps you find bills by subject and trace the progress of bills in the current session. Remember that if a bill fails to become law in one Congress it has to be reintroduced at the next Congress to be considered. The CCH *Congressional Index* also gives the voting records of congresspeople.

---

4 Note, *CIS Index to Unpublished Senate Committee Hearings 18th–88th Congress, 1823–1964* (1986), 5 vols. [More than 7,300 Senate transcripts on microfiche identified by Congress and Committee Code. e.g., (80) SFo-T.76].

9. *United States Statutes* includes individual laws, issued separately as slip laws, such as P.L. 76-82 (Public Law No. 82 of the 76th Congress). These are bound by year, with a subject and popular name index. To reference the laws, however, you should use the *U.S. Code*, which codifies the laws in force under title and section. There are subject and popular name indexes to the *U.S. Code*. At the foot of every section of law in the *Code* is a reference to the succession of public laws and amendments that led up to the present law (e.g., 75 Stat. 1325, meaning volume 75 of the *United States Statutes*, p. 1325).

10. The *Federal Register* (published daily, with monthly and annual indexes) gives the rules and regulations of federal agencies, which are cumulated in the *Code of Federal Regulations* (CFR) under title and part numbers. There is an index to the CFR. Presidential executive orders and proclamations are published in the *Federal Register* and cumulated in separate volumes.

11. *Treaties in Force* consists of a list of treaties and other international agreements of the United States that are in force. It appears annually, arranged by country and then by subject within the country. A paragraph description is given for each treaty, with reference to where the full text can be found (e.g., TIAS [U.S. State Dept. *Treaties and International Agreements Series*); 20 UST 456 [e.g., vol. 20 of the *US Treaties and Other International Agreements* (1950–) p. 456]; 80 Stat. 200 [e.g., vol. 80 of the U.S. Statutes, p. 200]). Historically, there is the U.S. State Department's *Subject Index of the Treaty Series and the Executive Agreement Series* (before July 1931).

12. *Government Reports and Announcements Index,* issued periodically, includes PB, AD, PS, and UB reports in the National Technical Information Service (NTIS) series. The *Nuclear Science Abstracts* lists report series from the Department of Energy (DOE), Energy Research Agency (ERA), and the International Nuclear Information System (INIS). The *STAR Index* (Scientific and Technical Aerospace Reports) carries documents of the National Aeronautics and Space Administration (NASA).

13. *Declassified Documents Quarterly Catalog* abstracts and indexes by subject documents made available to the public by U.S. agencies, such as the State Department, the National Security Council, the Central Intelligence Agency, and the White House. The documents on microfiche are found by an identifying number from the *Quarterly Catalog*.

    For federal documents kept not in the library, but in government agencies, a useful guide is *Legally Available U.S. Government Information as a Result of the Public Information Act* (1970): vol. 1. Department of Defense and the National Aeronautics and Space Administration, vol. 2. Other U.S. Government Agencies (M.J. Kerbec, ed.; Arlington, VA: Output Systems, 1970).

    Many documents are useful for research, such as court records, business records, and county records; Harry J. Murphy's *Where's What; Sources of Information for Federal Investigators* (Brookings Institute)[5] is a guide to these documents.

14. CIS *Index to U.S. Government Publications,* listing by subject and author, provides an identifying number that refers you to its companion volume, the *Abstract.* The *Abstract* provides the name of the issuing office or congressional committee with which the publication can be found in the library catalogue. The identifying number also guides you to the microfiche copy. The *Index* and *Abstract* are issued monthly and cumulated annually from 1970.

15. Commerce Clearing House (CCH) *Tax Guide* is a multivolumed, looseleaf service to the federal and state tax laws, organized by year. CCH also publishes the *Tax Cases* series (Prentice-Hall publishes a *Tax Guide* as well).

16. The Bureau of National Affairs (BNA) *Labor Reporter* is a comprehensive guide to labour court cases, arbitration cases, wage and hour cases, unfair labour practice cases, the regulations of federal labour agencies such as the Equal Employment Opportunities Agency, and state labour laws.

---

5 See also Craig T. Norback, *The Computer Invasion* (Van Nostrand Reinhold, 1981), to gain access to personal files in federal, state, and local governments.

For federal court cases generally, see the *Federal Reporter* and the *Federal Supplement*. For state court cases, see the *Reporter* and *Supplement* for each state, for example, the *New York State Reporter*.

The Internet gives you information on the U.S. Congress, its bills, statutes, roll call votes, committee information, status of legislation, the *Congressional Record*, and so on, under the rubric Thomas Legislative Information found on the Library of Congress home page (http://www.loc.gov).

British Government Publications

1. *Government Publications Index* lists government publications issued during the year, gives series and monograph numbers (particularly useful for finding the numbers of parliamentary command papers), and provides a subject index.
2. The *Parliamentary Papers* (catalogued as 'Great Britain, Parliament, *Sessional papers*') are much used for economic and social studies from 1800 to the present. Special indexes cover the nineteenth century. For the twentieth century, use the *Government Publications Index*. Less frequently used, but important, are the House of Lords Papers, from 1800, to which there are special subject indexes for the nineteenth century.
3. The *Numerical Finding List of British Command Papers Published 1833–1961/62*, by DiRoma and Rosenthal, lists, under parliamentary session, command papers by numbers and the corresponding volumes of the *Parliamentary Papers*. Documents librarians update it for their own libraries. After you find the number of the command paper in the *Government Publications Index*, you use the *Finding List* to locate the volume of the *Parliamentary Papers* in which the command paper is found.
4. *Parliamentary Debates* of both Houses are in one series with subject indexes to each session until 1935, when the Houses began issuing their debates separately.
5. *Parliamentary Journals,* issued from each House beginning in the sixteenth century, are used to trace legislation and reports.
6. For treaties, you can consult *Index to the British and Foreign State*

Papers, 1378–1873, 1873–1900, 1900–21, 1922–34, 1935–60, and so on.
7. Great Britain, Public Record Office, *Guide to the Records,* is a broad subject guide to manuscripts from the days of the British Emplre.

Other Governments

Other governments issue national bibliographies of their government publications on a monthly or annual basis.

Government gazettes report current decrees and laws.

International governments and organizations appear to use complicated document classification systems. Fortunately, finding the documents is relatively simple.

The United Nations

The UN publishes two distinct sets of publications: (1) sales publications, intended for sale to the general public, and (2) documents – mimeographed publications given agency classification numbers and distributed internally but available for public perusal.

Sales publications are included with their numbers, in annual lists issued by the UN. Because libraries do not catalogue UN sales publications, you must use these UN lists to find the sales number of a sales publication to request the item from the library. For example, the UN *Statistical Yearbook* for 1978 is listed chronologically in the UN lists under the statistical yearbook series; its sales number is E/F 79/XVII.1.

You look for the call number in the library catalogue under 'United Nations. Publications. Sales no. –' and copy this entry with the sales and call numbers on the request slip. For instance, in NYPL, 'XFB' is the call number for all UN sales number publications (see Figure 3.3). (The Roman Numeral XVII in the sales number differentiates the statistical yearbook series from other series.)

United Nations documents are indexed in the monthly *Index* to

Fig. 3.3

The New York
Public Library   Call number: XFB
ASTOR, LENOX AND TILDEN FOUNDATIONS

Author or
Periodical: United Nations Publications

Book Title: Sales no. E/F 1979. XVII. 1

Date/Vol. No.:

Correct and Legible Name and Address Required

Name   Mary Jackson

Address   31 Main St.

City   NY NY   Zip 10007

School or Business   Allardyce Inc.

Seat number:

72

form 28s

the documents of the general assemblies, committees, and special groups of the UN and affiliate agencies, which is cumulated annually beginning with 1950 (the 1950 volume includes the documents from 1946). Subject and country indexes give the document number with which you find the bibliographic entry for the document in the main section of the *Index*. With the year of the *Index* and the document number (i.e., 1977, A/AC.131/SR 290), you can find the document on microcard or microfiche; for recent years, libraries may still have the document on paper. Note that the documents of the UN's affiliate agencies, such as the Food and Agricultural Organization (FAO) and the UN Educational, Scientific and Cultural Organization (UNESCO), are found in this *Index*, but the sales publications of these affiliates are not found in the UN *Sales Publication* series – they are catalogued in the library catalogues like other books and serials.

Other international organizations, such as the Organization for Economic Co-operation and Development (OECD) and the Organization of American States (OAS), issue catalogues identifying their publications, but their approaches differ. For instance, because the OECD tends to publish in paper form, you can find its publications through the library catalogues, whereas the OAS tends to issue documents on microfiche, the numbers to which are found in indexes.

Newsbank has put the *Readex United Nations Index* on CD-ROM with selected full-text resolutions from the General Assembly, Security Council, and the Economic and Social Council appended to their respective bibliographic citations.

European Community Documents

The best guide to EC documentation is Ian Thomson's *Documentation of the European Communities*. The *SCAD Bulletin*, which has about 40 issues a year, is the best current bibliographical tool. The *Official Journal of the European Communities* comprises several series that are catalogued separately. The significant series are the *Legislation series* ('L' series), the *Information and Notices series* ('C' series), and the *Debates of the European Parliament*. There is an *Index to the Official Journal*.

The Commission of the European Communities publishes *COM Documents*, the main source for proposals and discussions of EC legislation. Some years are on microfiche and some are on paper, which requires libraries to compile finding aids to the microfiche numbers.

National Trade Data Bank (NTDB) on CD-ROM

As it becomes increasingly possible to store large quantities of information on a compact disc, numerous indexes are available on the CD-ROM monitors. Entire encyclopedias, catalogues, and telephone directories (as well as periodical indexes, to which we referred earlier) are available on CD-ROM for use in libraries and on your home computer. For example, a CD-ROM that gives you information from numerous publications in paper is the United States Commerce Department's National Trade Data Bank. It targets markets for exporters by giving monthly updates of international trade and economic information, such as government-sponsored market research by country and product, foreign interest and exchange rates, trade and investment statistics, lists of import-oriented foreign organizations, and so on. The information is found through two software packages: BROWSE and ROMWARE. BROWSE is structured as a series of pyramids that guide you from general to specific information. Under such categories as Source, Topic, Program, Subject, Title, you are led to more specific categories from which you can select detailed information. BROWSE uses Boolean indicators (AND, OR, NOT) so that, for example, from the PROGRAM you can select COUNTRY and specify 'Germany,' set the Boolean indicator to AND, and specify 'Electromechanical Hand Tools' OR 'Electron Tubes and Parts,' thus calling up a list of program sections with the appropriate pricing information.

ROMWARE is intended for the sophisticated user, allowing you to search for specific information across the entire data bank. This service is available by subscription over the Internet at http://www.stat-usa.gov/tradtest.nsf.

Microfiche Collections of Documents Made by Commercial Companies

A great many archival series and indexes to archives have been reproduced on microfiche by companies and sold to libraries that can afford them. If the library you are using does not have the fiche, you can search online to find which libraries do have it. All research libraries should keep files of brochures from the companies listing the collections microfiched.

The Chadwyck-Healey company, for instance, microfiched Great Britain, Foreign Office, *Registers and Indexes of Correspondence, 1793–1919*, from the collections in the Public Record Office. The only means of access to the correspondence and dispatches of the Foreign Office is through the contemporary handwritten *Registers* in the Reference Room of the Public Record Office. Since the *Registers* cannot be identified and retrieved without their Class List numbers, these numbers are added to each microfiche. The contemporary indexes are also reproduced on microfiche.

The *Registers* record the correspondence between the British government and its agents abroad. Statesmen, ambassadors, consuls, spies, and British travellers in every part of the world have reported on significant events to create an intelligence-gathering system that has become an important source of information about the political and economic history of many countries. The *Registers* were microfiched in 15 groups: (1) United States of America; (2) Asia and the Pacific; (3) Germany; (4) Russia, Prussia, and Central Asia; (5) Austria-Hungary, Balkans, and Greece; (6) Italy and Switzerland; (7) France; (8) Low Countires and Scandinavia; (9) Spain and Portugal; (10) Turkey and Egypt; (11) Africa and the Slave Trade; (12) Mexico and Central America; (13) South America; (14) The First World War and International Conferences; (15) Card Index 1906–19.

Of course, to see the actual reports you will have to visit the Public Record Office, Kew Gardens, London.

Other projects by Chadwyck-Healey provide the full document, such as its 'Radical Pamphlets in American Collections,' which consists of many thousands of pamphlets from the nineteenth and twentieth centuries.

Chadwyck-Healey also offers documents over the Internet to subscribers.

An important collection on microfiche is *Pamphlets in American History, 1716–1980* (Microfilming Corporation of America), consisting of over 17,000 titles based on the holdings of the University of Wisconsin and other libraries. Organized in five groups – each accompanied by a guide – with numerous subgroups, it includes in Group I, for example, subject series Revolutionary War (404 titles), Revolutionary War Biography (140), General Biography (2,579), Women (646), and Indians (1,519). In each guide, the numerically arranged citations are organized by subject series and then by accession number.

A further example of microform collections is the Harvester microfilm collection of street literature comprising 1,500 rare chapbooks – *Popular Literature in 18th and 19th Century Britain: The*

Robert White Collection of Chapbooks. It is Part 1 of a three-part series. Part 2 is the Sabine Baring-Gould and Thomas Crampton Collections from the British Library, which shifts focus from the chapbook pedlar's rural constituency to the mass market of the cities. Part 3 is the Barry Ono Collection of 'bloods' and penny dreadfuls.

The University Publications of America has issued countless valuable collections on American history on microfiche such as *U.S. Military Intelligence Reports: Surveillance of Radicals in the United States, 1917–1941.*

COOPERATIVE SYSTEMS AND INTERLIBRARY LOANS

A research library always has arrangements for borrowing books not in its collection from another research library, at the request of scholars. With the increase in the cost of purchasing and cataloguing books and the availability of telecommunication systems, research libraries now cooperate in the acquisition and lending of books and periodicals in highly organized systems. For instance, many research libraries in Europe and North America are members of the Research Libraries Group (RLG), which share their library resources through a Research Libraries Information Network (RLIN).

RLIN (Research Libraries Information Network)

For librarians and scholars, RLIN is a way to search a machine-readable database that includes not only the equivalent of their library's card catalogue, but also the catalogues of other member and user institutions, plus machine-readable cataloguing produced by the Library of Congress. As with a conventional card catalogue, searching can be done by personal name, corporate name, title, and subject heading. In addition, RLIN users can search by Library of Congress card number, local call number, International Standard Book Number (ISBN), International Standard Serial Number (ISSN), and several special indexes for films, maps, sound recordings, musical scores, and serials.

The RLIN Bibliographic File, which includes more than 30 million titles, is updated daily. Library readers use Eureka on the Web to locate the publications. You should select Simple Search when starting to use Eureka. You can search by keyword. Since there are many files to search, you choose Select a File for a list and description of other files you can search. Use Advanced Search to see more indexes and to combine different indexes. Word indexes for author, title, and subject appear only on the Advanced Search screen. If you want an article from a magazine or a section from a book, the library holding the material generally will photocopy the pages and send them to your requesting library.

RLIN also has citations to manuscript collections.

RLG has nonbibliographic databases such as the Medieval and Early Modern Data Bank (MEMDB), which provides scholars with an electronic reference library of information on the medieval and early modern period (from circa AD 800 to 1800), including medieval currency exchange quotations from Europe, Byzantium, the Levant, and North Africa, and information on wages, prices, demographics, property holdings, and so forth.

The Eureka terminal will find the materials if you experiment with combining keywords, but if you cannot find what you want you may ask the interlibrary loan librarian to find it using the original RLIN terminal, which requires a more complicated search procedure used only by some interlibrary loan librarians and cataloguers.

OCLC (Online Computer Library Center)

An access computer terminal, OCLC provides shared catalogue information for more than 37 million records in 370 languages from over 5,500 libraries and resource centres through the WorldCat database, which is located in most large libraries. Some libraries contract directly with OCLC; the majority of libraries participate through regional library networks. The Library of Congress is a member of OCLC. Several libraries of the City University of New York are hooked up with OCLC.

OCLC has implemented an online Interlibrary Loan Communications subsystem (a message-switching and record-keeping system). RLIN, UTLAS, and WLN have terminal-to-terminal message-switching capabilities with which they are developing online interlibrary loan modules. If your research library does not have an OCLC hookup, it usually can arrange for searches to be made on OCLC through another library.

UTLAS (University of Toronto Library Automation Systems)

Libraries contract directly with UTLAS for services. One consortium of libraries, UNICAT/TELECAT, contracts directly on behalf of its members.

WLN (Washington [State] Library Network)

Unlike the others, WLN is not trying to become a national network, but rather is encouraging groups of libraries outside the Pacific Northwest to replicate or transfer the WLN system by purchasing its software and installing it on local computer systems.

Library Consortiums

Local bibliographic systems in municipalities such as Chicago, San Francisco, Washington, DC, Rochester, and in other countries have developed cooperative information and user programs regionally. Their Internet home pages are linked with the major libraries in their areas. You may find them on the Internet by entering 'library council' on search engines such as Yahoo. Some provide access to library home pages in their regions and thus to library catalogues online; others, such as the Council of Federal Libraries in Canada, list federal libraries, personnel, and other information. A major example of these systems is METRO.

METRO (Metropolitan New York Library Council) System

The New York Public Library helped develop a cooperative acquisitions and users system with libraries in Greater Metropolitan

New York called METRO. Publications obtained through METRO are catalogued in the online catalogues of the member libraries; the call number designates which library has the item. You ask a librarian for a METRO card, which introduces you to the other library and allows you to consult the publication. METRO also has a Route Messenger Service that makes deliveries between four public library systems (Brooklyn, New York, Queens, Westchester), three school library systems (New York City, Putnam-Northern Westchester, and Yonkers), and METRO libraries located in New York City. METRO also runs a Free Interchange of Photocopies Program. You may expect these and other types of services in other regions.

METRO's Internet address (www.metro.org) can link you to the home pages and catalogues of its 300 library members in the five boroughs and Westchester, from which you can link onto the catalogues of libraries and home pages in other regions. It represents over 1,200 libraries of all kinds. You will also see its newsletter *@METRO*, online since 1997, in which you will find, under 'Net Notes,' links to such items as 'Cyndi's List of Genealogy Sites on the Internet' (www.CyndisList.com) and 'Culture Finder' (www.CultureFinder.com), which covers over 300,000 theatre, music, opera, dance, and visual arts events nationwide, and where viewers can buy tickets per date and city.

Before 1997, METRO published a monthly newsletter, *For Reference*, which reported on interesting new acquisitions such as:

- Canterbury, Eng. (Province), *Registers of the Archbishops of Canterbury in Lambeth Palace Library*, 37 vols. in 20 35-mm microfilm reels (administrative transactions and official correspondence from 1279 through 1645).
- New York Philharmonic Symphony Society, *Program Notes, Ist–132nd season, 1842–1974* (32 reels of microfilm).
- U.S. Committee on Fair Employment Practice, *Selected Documents of Records ... 1941–1946* (1970); 213 reels (useful for research in social and labour history).

It also alerted you to special collections such as CORECAT, a microfiche catalogue of the major theological libraries, and *Index Iconologicus*, 400 microfiches, compiled by the Duke University Art Department, 1980.

The titles to publications listed in *For Reference* were entered in the catalogues of the member libraries such as CATNYP (NYPL) and Bob Cat Plus (New York University). But in the early years some were not entered, and thus you should refer to the METRO CAP catalogue of expensive research titles purchases, 1972–9, kept in member libraries (it includes more than 14,000 individual titles; most of the entries are unduplicated in libraries in the region).

CRL (Center for Research Libraries, Chicago)

CRL is an international centre for research materials with a collection of more than 5 million volumes, including newspapers, archival materials, and government records in microfilm. CRL has a 17–volume catalogue of its holdings, available in large research libraries, and has an online catalogue that can be accessed through the Internet (http://www.crl.uchicago.edu). It makes available its research sources to users everywhere. If the research library that you are using is not a member of CRL, a transaction fee is charged for each request that CRL fills.

CRL can acquire PhD dissertations of foreign universities that are not represented in *Dissertations Abstracts International*. If CRL does not have the dissertation on hand, it can purchase and lend it. The time it takes to acquire a dissertation varies from six weeks to several months.

CRL has an arrangement with the British Lending Library that sends articles from foreign journals in the sciences and social sciences, if you cannot find the journal in North America.

CRL purchases printed materials on microform collected by the cooperating microfilm projects of South Asia, Southeast Asia, Latin America, and Africa. A copy of CRL's microfiche catalogue of these projects is kept in a library's microforms division.

For other CRL services, see the *Handbook of the Center for Research Libraries* or check it out on the Internet.

European Services

In Europe, each country has a bibliographic centre to which interlibrary loan requests are sent. For instance, the British Libraries Bibliographic Centre in Yorkshire receives requests from libraries in every area of the United Kingdom, searches its bibliographic files for a library that has the desired publication, and forwards the loan request to it.

The national bibliographic centres in Europe arrange for the lending of publications between European countries. In North America the National Library in Ottawa and major research centres in the United States cooperate in interlibrary loans. But there is no lending for private research between continents. You must pay for photocopies of the items, which the foreign library forwards to you through your research centre.

Catalogue computer search services have sprung up in every European country. For instance, British Libraries Automated Information System (Blaise) contains British books published since 1950, and American and other books catalogued by the Library of Congress since 1968. The Bibliothèque Nationale has a similar search service, Télésystèmes. Many of these systems also carry periodical databases. For instance, Télésystèmes has FRANCIS, an index to periodical articles, books, and other publications in two sections: one for the humanities, the other for social sciences.

VIDEOTEX

Whereas online services provide reference to secondary sources or published literature, videotex presents primary information from a mainframe computer. You select it on the screen from a seemingly unlimited number of frames of information in either text or graphic form. Transmission – by satellite, cable, optical fibre, or telephone links – is displayed on a modified black-and-white or colour TV set, a multi-use terminal, or a dedicated monitor. Videotex system operators act only as common carriers. Business and nonprofit organizations provide the information. It is most popular in France, where it goes under the names of *Teletel* and *Minitel.* In Germany it is called *Bildschirmtext* and has been used in the Bavarian school system with a telephone information system giving access to several databases wherever the large academic database networks are too costly for school use. In the United Kingdom it is called the *Prestel* system and in Canada it is the *Telidon* system. In the United States it is run by *CompuServe.* Videotex has evolved into an interactive communication service using electronic bulletin boards and electronic mail, but its transmission difficulties have kept it from developing. When satellite transmission to rooftop antennas becomes practical, videotex should become popular.

LEVELS OF RESEARCH – SUMMING UP

If you want current information or information specific to an institution, either call library reference or try the Internet.

If you intend to search a large body of literature for a source that is hard to find or for as many references to a subject as you can get, you will use the online retrieval systems in the library. They reduce a search that would take days of going through printed sources to a matter of minutes.

If you are searching for a specific topic and, at the same time, remain open to related themes, it is often easier to use the printed sources. When you are doing historical research, often only printed sources are available.

Chapter 4

Research in Depth

There are two kinds of researchers. Some work within a deadline and others search until they get the full answer. The first type are responding to the needs or the demands of schools; the searchers of knowledge are usually writing the books and essays of the future or laying the groundwork for other creative works or inventions. The gap between them is enormous. Let us deal first with the harried businesswoman and the frightened college student writing a term paper.

The businesswoman may wish to know whether she should open her retail store to more merchandise. She is interested in the state of her competition, in the changes in her neighbourhood, in the general salability of certain products, and in the prospects for small business generally. She knows enough to come to the business section of the library.

In the business division, she faces row upon row of reference books and tries to remember what questions to ask the librarian. Her time is very limited – not more than two hours every day for one week. She wants current information only; therefore the publications should be quickly accessible. The recent census material is on the open reference shelves. The census of retail trade informs her about her competition; the censuses of population and housing (especially the census tracts) tell her of the social characteristics of her neighbourhood; the current industrial reports tell her of the number and value of products manufacturers; the latest volumes of the periodical index *Predicasts* forecast growth rates of industries in the economy generally. She turns to the latest *Funk and Scott Index* to find articles about her industry and new products, and, because she is pressed for time, she restricts herself to those articles in current issues that can be fetched quickly from the current periodical shelves.

If willing to spend more time, she would select articles from older issues, find their call numbers in the catalogue, and, while waiting for their delivery, look through special bibliographical indexes such as the *Cumulative Index of the Conference Board*, an organization that monitors and publishes reports on business and labour conditions.

This reader quickly analysed her situation with questions that could be dealt with by reference books on the open shelves (found with the help of librarians), and came away within the required time with enough information on which to base a decision.

Another reader with a similar question may begin looking in the library catalogue by subject heading, find nothing relevant, turn in frustration to general periodical indexes such as *Readers' Guide*, and search through several years for a few likely references that turn out to be out of date and of no specific help on his subject. 'A whole day wasted!' he mutters, and returns to his business none the wiser. He failed to organize his problem into a set of distinct questions, and being unfamiliar with the many sources published by governments, he did not begin his research with the right reference materials. Also, he failed to understand that his time limitations meant he should seek only current materials available on open reference or periodical shelves – and that he should ask for the guidance that librarians are there to give him.

The student term paper writer, on the other hand, usually must do historical research and use the catalogues and periodical indexes. But he also is pressed for time. Required to write 25 pages or more on, say, Charles Dickens' place in the development of the novel of social realism, the student must analyse the problem in terms of the availability of information. He must rely on

what has already been written. He looks in the printed book catalogue of Library of Congress subject headings, which are standard to all computer catalogue systems, and finds the subject
heading of 'DICKENS, CHARLES,' which will lead him on the
computer catalogue to bibliographies about Dickens' work and
the biographies about him. He finds the subject heading 'REAL-
ISM IN LITERATURE, ENGLISH' and types it into the computer
catalogue for bibliographies and several good books on the subject. If there is any difficulty in locating a specific subject, he
should ask a librarian to point out other possible subject headings in that library's catalogue.

The bibliographies, especially if annotated, help him assess
which books are most useful and give references to periodical
articles, thus saving the time of poring over years of periodical
indexes. Also, he looks under the subject heading for social
aspects of nineteenth-century England and selects one or two
comprehensive treatments. With the books in hand (they have
arrived in batches at his seat as he continues to do research in the
catalogue), he refers to the indexes in the back, reads very selec-
tively the pages indicated, and puts down the bibliographic citations of his sources in his notes. If the bibliographies fail to
provide him with sufficient references to literary criticism, he
may request critical works on English literature of the period,
found, again, through subject headings in the library catalogue.

Another student, required to write about George Eliot's atti-
tude toward women's liberation, investigates recent biographies
and searches through the past few years of periodical indexes
online, such as the *Humanities Index*. Only as a last resort will she
turn to the more general subject headings in the catalogue,
because the nature of the inquiry is topical and more likely to be
found in periodical essays.

Without reflecting on the relation of the problem to the ave-
nues of information in each case, the students might have started
in the wrong direction and spent many hours in fruitless
research. Poor research can hurt the businessperson financially
and the student academically, but for the searcher of truth in the
long term it can bring disaster.

APPROACHES TO RETRIEVABLE INFORMATION

The Researchers

Are these the men and women of stooped shoulder and weary gait, whose lungs are clogged with library air and whose faces and hands are stained with bibliographic rash, the pursuers of dusty books and ancient parchment? No, they are the young and eager, hopeful of finding fame through some area of lore opened to them only through the riches of the library. Or they may be the solace-seekers in refuge for a few hours from the brutal, unmannered world of the twenty-first century. They all are our thinkers and, in a sense, our mentors, for what they write shapes our lives. We will analyse their approaches to their subjects in detail.

For the point of view of a famous researcher, let us quote C. Wright Mills' 'On Intellectual Craftsmanship' in *Reader in Research Methods for Librarianship* (1970): 'Seldom does the literature illuminate the sheer joy and intellectual adventure of research.'

The Historical Approach

Perhaps the nineteenth century is the period most popular with today's scholars; in terms of analysing for retrievable information, it differs tremendously from, say, the sixteenth or the late twentieth.

At the beginning of the nineteenth century, the innovations in paper making and printing allowed life to be recorded with a fullness not possible earlier. The records of the time, therefore, are quite extensive, but, because of the infancy and inexperience of most libraries, they are not available now in all research libraries; the researcher faces the problem of locating all the publications to which he or she has references. On the other hand, the researcher into the sixteenth century is more concerned with locating manuscript collections, particularly letters of the period, and is confined to specific special collections or to manuscript and autograph dealers. The researcher into the late twentieth century faces the problem of selecting only what is absolutely essential from the mass of printed material available and, at the same time, avoiding any kind of preselection that bibliographic and online services may impose.

Let us, for the sake of illustration, follow a researcher whose subject is a little-known person of the nineteenth century. This person was a soldier and an inventor, and he wrote for periodicals. He had an Italian name but was English. The researcher had come across a pamphlet of his instructing the English in how to use canes in street fighting. Who was this man? An autobiography is easily located in the catalogue but it avoids in-depth treatment, preferring to emphasize the glamour of adventure. The *Dictionary of National Biography* has no entry for him. The indexes to *Notes and Queries* refer to a query about him in the late nineteenth century and a reply from an old gentleman who remembered meeting him at a dinner party 40 years earlier.

At this point the researcher must think about the time period of his subject. The first half of the nineteenth century buzzed with ideas for inventions discussed in the science and art magazines of the day. The researcher finds by subject heading in the library catalogue that the *Mechanics' Magazine* is a standard source for that time. He looks through the indexes to the *Mechanics' Magazine* of London and finds numerous references to the man and to his ideas for inventions. This man's association with other people is mentioned. A search for the papers of the most prominent of his associates through application to the British Historical Manuscripts Commission brings the researcher to a batch of his letters in the papers of a nobleman preserved in London University. This correspondence leads to other collections of personal papers, all of which reveal the man's politics, deeds, and psychology.

The time was one of great unrest. By checking the guides to manuscript collections of the period's political and labour societies papers, the researcher is able to begin studying the character and politics of the man and his opponents.

The Geographic Approach

Delving into the lives of the man's contemporaries, the researcher

discovers that one of the man's daughters married into a prominent family whose name appears as the subject of a family study in
the *British Library Catalogue*. The study devotes two pages to the
hero's background. With facts from the half-completed autobio-
graphical study of the man's military career, the researcher turns
to a geographic approach. He searches for books and articles
describing the wars and military campaigns in which the hero took
part, and keeps a sharp lookout for footnotes that inform him in
which foreign archives papers about the campaigns have been
stored. He pores over directories to genealogical archives, and,
having corresponded with archivists and located where important
materials are held, researches in those foreign archives for all the
papers relevant to the politics, social background, associates, and
other aspects of the hero. He may even visit the places where the
hero is known to have lived and imagine, with help from local
archives, how the scenes must have looked to the hero.

The Subject Approach

The researcher then comes up with a handful of subjects or
themes to pursue more deeply. That is, he must now read into the
background of the wars, inventions, and themes that he finds significant, to understand their origin and why the hero became
involved with them. The result of his research should bring the
eventual reader of his book to an understanding of the man and
his time that the man himself could never have had.

Other Approaches

The interpretive approach is used when all the facts are available,
such as in the archives of a company. The researcher's interpretation of the company's history depends on her general knowledge
of the company's competitors, the business climate, and the acu-
men of the entrepreneurs. If the researcher must discuss a period
of the literature, her interpretive approach should be from one of
several possible points of view – the symbolic, the biographical,
the social-political, the literary-historical, or some other. From

here, she can readily discover the availability of retrievable information through bibliographies and the subject entries in library catalogues.

The exclusionary or renunciatory approach requires the researcher to choose, from a great many, one overriding message she wishes to communicate from a plethora of material. The filmmaker of a 90–minute film on the life of Picasso admitted that renunciation was her guideline whereby she ruthlessly excised interesting facets of Picasso's life to give the film shape and meaning. It is an approach adopted by modern-day historians. Unlike Gibbon, they strive not for the whole picture, but merely to contribute to an overall view that later generations may form. Their contributions, however, are satisfying and appear complete to their contemporaries. They therefore research only those aspects that enhance or illuminate the point of view they wish to express.

WHEN TO USE BIBLIOGRAPHIES, INDEXES, BOOKS, PERIODICALS, AND MANUSCRIPTS AS EXEMPLIFIED BY SUBJECT AREA

General Knowledge

Sometimes researchers must use all the departments of a research library to track down a subject. The foregoing example of the Englishman who was soldier, inventor, and writer is a case in point. The military and literary books and articles would be found in the humanities division, whereas a search into his inventions would be done through periodical indexes in the science and the patents divisions.

Another example of a search for general knowledge is the professor gathering material for a book on the mosquito. Like the mosquito, information about it and its effect on humans could appear in any room in the library. The professor spent many hours hunting down government publications in the Economic and Public Affairs Division in the New York Public Library, and, in fact, used all the divisions including Rare Books and Manuscripts. Since NYPL does not hold medical books, he spent months in the New York Academy of Medicine Library, which is open to the public. For the legal implications of mosquitoes, to be found in legal publications too specialized for NYPL, he visited the New York University Law Library with a METRO card. After three years, the professor had written three shopping bags full of manuscript and was looking for a publisher.

Let us, for the sake of presenting a case closer to the average, follow a freelance writer who is under a long-term contract to a publisher to produce a definitive book on the continent of Atlantis. The subject will lead him into mythology, archaeology, literature, voyages of discovery, studies of cultures, economic history, biography, and fields he could not imagine when he commences his research. He does not know how he will present the subject, but, from what he supposed about it, he begins to analyse it in terms of where he can get the information.

He chooses two areas of reading: the mythology of Atlantis and the literature of explorers who have looked for it. These two areas seem to balance one another, as part of the mythology comes from historians of the ancient world and the voyages of discovery are based on facts gleaned from mythology. They will touch on other areas of research, of course, but these new references the researcher must note and put aside, regardless of their fascination, until he has exhausted his research in the first two areas. No doubt, he has already determined that the archaeological will be his third approach, but whatever follows that depends on the revelations of his research.

He begins by consulting the subject headings in the library catalogues for works on mythology and narrations of discovery. These give him background, bibliographic references, and scores of ideas. He turns to periodical literature, starting with the latest indexes and working backwards. By starting with the latest articles in both fields, he may come across references to earlier articles that were not indexed. The only index to nineteenth-century periodicals with any claim to comprehensiveness is *Poole's Index*. Many other periodicals kept their own indexes. Haskell's guide (*A Checklist of Cumulative Indexes to Periodicals in the New York Public*

Library) is important for its listing of French and German periodical indexes; a searcher, to research such a subject, should read a few modern languages.

A good research library should have complete runs of foreign periodicals or be able to borrow microfilm reels of periodicals from other libraries.

The monotony of research may be felt after a time, so that the researcher who began with two fields may be grateful that he can change from mythology to personal adventure and back again. The bulk of personal adventure probably remains unpublished, but if it were at all important, it might be located in manuscript collections throughout Europe and America. The researcher may welcome this respite from his reading as he looks through directories to archives and libraries for various countries, catalogues and guides to special collections, and bibliographies of works and manuscripts on exploration through the centuries.

He writes to the archivists of special collections he wishes to visit. This correspondence may lead him to other collections, the existence of which he could not have known about, and to scholars in the field who, for the most part, will respond to his queries with useful suggestions. By this point, he has only touched the tip of the iceberg.

His visits to manuscript collections bring him a wealth of material, all of which he may spend some weeks assimiliating before he goes on to the archaeological approach. As any casual reader of periodical literature knows, there have been several discoveries of 'Atlantis' in recent years. The archaeological reports of these expeditions are published in the papers of archaeological societies; personal reports of the expedition members may be lodged with the organizations that sponsored the expeditions. No doubt, the researcher will have noted down many archaeological sources from his primary reading. He may wish to find biographical information about expedition leaders to assess their motivations. Major newspapers often provide such information, and local newspapers from an archaeologist's birthplace sometimes provide interesting facts found nowhere else. Through the membership lists of professional organizations, the researcher may locate archaeologists for correspondence or interviews, though this type of research is best left to last, when the researcher feels he knows everything he needs to know to ask pertinent questions. Visits to the archaeological sites, however, may be considered important at any time during the research, because the researcher will find the necessity of keeping his reading (which gives him an abstract view of the subject) in touch with the reality.

A study of the cultures, religions, and philosophies of peoples contemporaneous with the archaeological sites may be helpful at this point. Through the subject entries in the library catalogues and standard encyclopedias, the researcher locates basic readings, but he may have to visit special libraries like the New York Union Theological Seminary Library, which is open to the public, to find the most informative material.

By comparing the artefacts from the site with the concepts of surrounding cultures, including the economic and legal aspects, the researcher may be able to interpret the culture in question and assess its discoverers' claims that it is the missing Atlantis. The researcher must constantly interpret the facts, as well as the validity of claims and counterclaims. Sometimes he must go back over his reading to make a reassessment. His notes, kept either on index cards or in notebooks, if sufficiently explicit, can save him much precious time. Also helpful is a special notebook in which he records his impressions from his research as he goes along.

Always, by the way, *keep complete bibliographic citations on every source* – down to the page number.

There is probably literature that evaluates the various Atlantis sites in terms of mythological or ancient description. The researcher should save the works of these commentators to read at the end of his research so as not to be influenced by it and to be able to argue authoritatively with it. Also, these references may provide insights or further leads that he can now chase down quickly and easily.

Humanities

Research in the humanities is largely interpretive but based on the knowledge of fundamental facts that may require the researcher to delve into several disciplines. A PhD candidate searching for the true significance of the poetry of Alfred Lord Tennyson may have to read the works of philosophers with influence in his day, biographies of the Tennyson family, and technical works on the phenomenon of memory so implicit in Tennyson's work. A thorough knowledge of the poetic works of Tennyson's immediate predecessors and contemporaries, in particular of Wordsworth, is a prerequisite to a study of Tennyson's poetry.

The researcher, therefore, would begin by consulting the bibliographies of the works of the poets and selecting the best critical works. She would consult the *Dissertations Abstracts* to see if research similar to what she plans has already been done, or if other dissertations may be of help to her. She works her way through a study of the poems she already appreciates by reading the poetry more carefully, the poet's biography, and the critics' judgments, and searching out the poet's techniques through background reading.

Literary interpretation is a slow process. After reading for a couple of years and attempting to express in writing her insights into the poetry gained from her reading, the researcher feels that she has entered the mind of Tennyson and is awake to his sensibilities. She finds the greatest delight in being able to show how erroneous were the judgments of previous critics; it makes the bond between Tennyson and herself seem stronger.

Although after the initial period of research the researcher does not consult the library catalogue as frequently, she regards the library as an essential support that at any time could present her with new literary works and articles relevant to her quest. For this reason she visits the current periodical room for literary magazines and review papers, such as the *Times Literary Supplement.* By this time the librarians in the humanities division may become aware of her field of research and draw her attention to recent publications. The library becomes her 'home away from home.' For further discussion of the route to productive research in the humanities, see Charles S. Singleton, *Interpretation, Theory and Practice* (Baltimore: Johns Hopkins, 1969).

Social Sciences

In the late nineteenth century the social sciences began to over-
take the humanities in importance and relevance to the world
around us. Research libraries do not reflect this change of status
because their role is historical as well as topical, but they have had
to devote an increasingly larger amount of shelf space in the
stacks to social science publications, since the space provided in
the social science departments was swamped long ago.

Social science subjects can be interdisciplinary; for example,
the voting habits of the English, as political science, touches on
economic history statistics and sociology. They can also be singu-
lar, such as econometric forecasting techniques. Social sciences
have also laid claim to subject fields traditionally conceived as
part of the humanities. Law, for instance, is related in many ways
to various social science compartments: housing law is central to
the socioeconomic struggle between landlords and tenants; con-
sumer law concerns the people versus the retailers; sociologists
deal every day with family court law, civil rights law, criminal law,
and so on; international law relates to economists and political
scientists; labour law relates to personnel managers, labour orga-
nizers, and contract negotiators. The same can be said of history
and philosophy: economic and political-social history are sup-
planting the general history books, and the economic-sociologi-
cal changes in philosophy, with the influence of Hegel,
Feuerbach, and Marx, have virtually revolutionized the subject as
a social science.

As a consequence of the feverish and exciting intellectual activity taking place in all these fields, the numerous periodical
indexes offer woefully inadequate coverage. The online data services merely give faster access to the indexes. A large part of social
sciences publications, because of either their ephemeral nature
or their political point of view, are overlooked by librarians and
their colleagues the indexers and abstracters. The researcher in
the social sciences, therefore, must scrutinize the back pages of
periodicals for advertisements or references to publications
unknown to him or to the library and locate specialized libraries

that are likely to have collected them. For publications of the political left, for example, certain church libraries can provide significant literature found nowhere else.

As an example of social sciences research, let us watch a political economist develop a case study to illustrate his theory about how technological diffusion (the disseminating of an invention) takes place.

The case study is the development of the automobile, which was invented in England in the 1820s by Goldsworthy Gurney but was not successfully diffused until the 1890s. The researcher wants to find the reasons for the delay.

First, he notes what the *Dictionary of National Biography* says about Goldsworthy Gurney and looks up the references given by the article about him. Since Goldsworthy was a Cornishman, he looks in Boase's *Bibliotheca Cornubiensis* and finds a long list of writings by Goldsworthy. In them Goldsworthy refers to parliamentary committees, the reports and evidence of which the researcher finds through the indexes to the *Sessional Papers* of the British House of Commons for the nineteenth century.

Finding that the steam automobile was repressed by parliament, the researcher searches through the *Journals* of the Lords and Commons for the bills introduced on its behalf and against it throughout the century. Through the indexes to parliamentary debates he discovers who is for the steam carriage and who is against it; he discovers that the *Mirror of Parliament* records the votes on important bills, that *Dod's Parliamentary Companion* gives biographical sketches of parliamentarians, and that the railway manuals list railway directors who are members of parliament. He returns to the library catalogue for books on the early railway and their entrepreneurs, and on English banking, English investment abroad, and Belgian and French banking in railways, which sprang up in the wake of British export of capital and machinery to those countries.

He finds that by alternating his research between the political-economic forces and the men who led them, he has developed a good idea of the class factions that favoured the railway over the automobile, but he needs a better idea of their motivation, which he feels only manuscript material can offer. He searches through the Great Britain Historical Records Commission's lists of manuscript acquisitions, which are annual listings of private papers turned over to county archives. Here he finds papers relevant to his themes and writes to the archives in question to ascertain their size and learn more about their subject matter.

(*Always write before visiting archives*, to forewarn the archivist, to make sure the papers have not been transferred, to be sure they relate to what you want, and to learn the hours and days the archives are open.)

While in England, the researcher consults the *British Library Catalogue*, including its special subject-heading book catalogues, which are excellent tools for locating books of the early nineteenth century, surpassed only by the subject-heading book catalogue of the Library of the London School of Economics, which he also consults. The latter library has an excellent collection of German and French economic books of the period that the researcher finds invaluable for background information to his theme.

The mass of information is now immense and the researcher has not touched the periodical literature. After chancing on the papers of the capitalist entrepreneur behind Gurney's automobile in a county archives and the papers of another early automobilist in a library of one of the colleges of London University, he must try to establish the relationship of the particular entrepreneurs to the changing society of the Industrial Revolution. This he cannot do without an economic theory, which begins to evolve from his findings as he reflects on the meaning of the economic and political factionalism. He reads the economics of technological diffusion, the readings for which he finds from the library catalogue's subject heading, and the *Index to Economic Articles*. The more he reads, the more he discovers that only Marxist economics has the analytical tools to explain the suppression of the automobile, but, because Marxist economics has not developed a theory of technological diffusion, he must develop one from his research within the Marxist economic framework.

One cannot research a theory; however, one can hope to

absorb a theory or philosophy by reading the works of its progenitor and its commentators. In the case of the researcher, this must be done when he is relaxing from the strain of his concentrated research.

He discovers bibliographies given as reference sources in books on automobiles in France, the petroleum engine, and its inventor Gottfried Daimler, which lead him to significant material in the Bibliothèque Nationale and the Archives Nationales in Paris.

Through a study of the price wars over petroleum among the Rockefellers, Rothschilds, and Nobels, he discovers why the petroleum automobile was promoted by the end of the century and, through a study of the changing class structure in France, he understands why the automobile was allowed to be diffused widely.

By this time he has developed a sixth sense of where material may be found. From Haskell's guide to periodical indexes, he is able to pick out the European magazines and time periods most useful to him. He can tell by the title of a book if it is likely to be sufficiently useful.

While writing his book, he will come upon small lacunae in his research that the library's collection can fill and he will stumble on information in the new issues of periodicals.

Since he is writing about automobiles and railways, he will have had to visit the science division to read about their construction and their workings throughout the nineteenth century.

Sciences

Most science collections are set up for the use of knowledgeable scientists. The New York Public Library's Science and Technology Research Center, however, is prized for making science accessible to the beginning student and carrying him or her through to the most sophisticated works. The inventor of xerography, for example, taught himself the sciences of mechanics and chemistry there.

Much of scientific research depends on searching the periodical literature such as the *Applied Science and Technology Index*. With the coming of computerization, this search for references has become sophisticated and, consequently, is used by scientists whose knowledge allows them to research at a high level.

A researcher in the textile industry, for instance, is looking for the latest scientific techniques, which he finds only through reading articles by a writer working in the trade or maintaining a close relationship with it. The periodical indexes do not index all the periodicals, especially newspapers, which the researchers must go through issue by issue. The *Gale Directory of Publications* gives him the title of trade periodicals, and the *Standard Directory of Periodicals* lists magazines by subject field.

The NYPL Patents Collection records all patents taken out anywhere in the world and is consulted by inventors who depend on a knowledge of the past and of the changing social conditions that may allow new concepts of construction or the discovery of new metals to make viable an invention that has lain in the Patents Books for years.

Research in science, however, can lead to the in-depth study of one or several of its many disciplines that requires research in specialized libraries. A directory to guide the researcher to these libraries is *Directory of Special Libraries and Information Centers* (Gale).

Special Collections

Although rare book and manuscript collections have been incorporated into research libraries' Web-accessible catalogues to a certain degree, you will find that the holdings of special collections in research and university libraries have been photocopied in book catalogues and distributed widely to other libraries. Directories of special collections classify them by subject so that the researcher first finds their names and locations and then looks in the research library catalogue for a listing of the book catalogues of whatever special collections he or she wishes to see. For example, New York Historical Society's card catalogue of manuscripts of old New York State, including the colonial days, is in book form.

As for what these special collections comprise, let us, as an example, look at the special collections of the New York Public Library.

The Rare Book Room

The Rare Book Room identifies rare books as monographs or serials published in Europe before 1601, in England before 1641, in the Americas before 1801, or modern fine printing. Being scarce does not usually qualify a publication for this collection if it was published after that date; such books are kept in the general stack area unless they are considered particularly valuable. A significant exception is the collection of modern fine printing – private press books designed by such important figures as Bruce Rogers, and books issued by distinguished book clubs. Researchers in rare books depend much on bibliographies in their subject fields, although there is a rare book card catalogue with subject entries. Rare printed books are valued for their artefactual as well as their textual interest. They are consulted not only for the information they give but for the style of calligraphy or printing, the texture of paper, and the method of binding, which inform us of the society in which they were produced and of the school of printing or period of artistry to which they belong.

Textual research is fundamental to the training of a scholar. For example, the methodology of textual research is taught at Oxford University, which awards successful students with a BLitt degree, a prerequisite for the Oxford PhD, regardless of the number of PhDs a student may have attained elsewhere.

Textual criticism has several aims. A researcher who hopes to lecture on the political factionalism among Tibetan religious orders may have to consult the book manuscripts of ancient Tibet on early religious tenets in the Rare Book Room. Other scholars compare the various texts of an author's work, both in manuscript and published forms, to trace his or her artistic development, or to establish a definitive text when an editor took liberties in preparing the work for publication.

On the subject of discovering influences on artists, Lord Tennyson provides us with a good example of a poet who, when his early poetry was strongly criticized, refused to publish for years and reworked his poems. For instance, the versions of 'The Lotus Eaters' published in 1833 and in 1842 differ markedly. The textual critic studies Tennyson's many drafts and editorial corrections in the poems throughout the years and researches the events and emotions of the poet's personal life and the social changes he lived through to understand the changes in the poem.

Variorum texts, on the other hand, carry all the changes in the text made by the author (or editors) and therefore require most students to study only the printed editions.

Years ago the textual critic reprinted her idea of the pure or best version of the poem with one or two variants in brackets, but in recent years, under the influence of American scholarship, poems have been reproduced with all variants in the margins of the same page. This is called the *workshop approach*, meaning that all the word tools that were used to construct the poem may be seen at once to give a comprehensive view of the artist's creative development.

Such a study involves the discipline of linguistics and a profound knowledge of the culture. The researcher should collect all the variants of the work in question and then read the correspondence of the artist. Published biographies and critical works of the artist can lead the researcher to collections of unpublished correspondence, but she must query any likely special manuscript collections as well. In the course of researching an artist's life, the researcher may be led to manuscripts of court trials and probate records in the Public Record Office. She must chase down every clue promising revelation until she is satisfied that she has a thorough knowledge of her subject. Then she searches out the book reviews in the periodicals of the day, and peruses them to give herself a feeling for the times.

Literature

Aside from collecting the printed works and correspondence of authors, special literary collections like the Berg or Pforzheimer Collections at the New York Public Library collect the handwritten and typewritten manuscripts of their books. When I saw the typescript of D.H. Lawrence's novel *Kangaroo* in the Berg Collection, I was surprised by its clean look because I knew that he had written it at top speed in a short time. Recently, however, I read that he always sent his work to be typed by others, and consequently, his handwritten manuscript with the corrections he made before it reached the typist alone would reveal his method of working. Revised typescripts, though, like Virginia Woolf's in the same collection, do tell such a story. The library purchases these manuscripts or receives them as gifts from the authors, their heirs, or collectors. Sometimes, as in the case of the letters and manuscripts of the poet W.H. Auden, a complicated court case is fought over their custody. In Auden's case, the poet left his papers to a friend, who in turn left them to NYPL's Berg Collection. After the friend died, a court ruled in favour of the Berg Collection as the legitimate recipient of the papers and against other claimants.

Just as in the Rare Book Room, where we find scholars at work on variorum editions of older texts, we might find scholars at work in the Berg or Pforzheimer Collections on textual criticism, or find both, on odd days, in Manuscripts and Archives.

Manuscripts

From large collections of material such as the papers of the American Loyalists on their losses from the Revolutionary War to single autograph letters (e.g., a note from the nineteenth-century poet George Foster, 'Yankee Doodle will meet you for lunch'), the Manuscripts and Archives section reaches out for all subjects. It has its own card catalogue and its own typewritten guides to particular collections. Manuscripts and Archives is especially useful for diaries, which can provide unique descriptions of a period the researcher hopes to understand. It may house all the papers of a particular personality such as the New York socialist politician of the first half of the twentieth century, Norman Thomas.

Some manuscript libraries specialize in particular subjects. For instance, the Schomburg Center for Research in Black Culture has a good collection of Haitian manuscripts, and collections from the Caribbean and from New York's Harlem. The Library's Billy Rose Theatre Collection at Lincoln Center has prompt books, correspondence of theatre people, old newspaper clippings, playbills, and photographs – all of which are useful to a researcher.

Finding the whereabouts of correspondence can be difficult. *Hamer's Guide to Archives and Manuscripts in the United States* and the *National Union Catalog of Manuscript Collections* (Library of Congress), issued periodically from 1959, name the library where the correspondence is kept and the number of items, but these merely touch on the great number of archives. The National Archives in Ottawa, Canada, issues reports on its collections and allows researchers to keep materials after working hours so that they may work through the night on their subject. In Britain, the Historical Manuscripts Research Centre in Quality Lane provides an immensely valuable service in locating manuscripts for researchers. Indeed, Europeans are working together to collect, preserve, and publish guides to their archives. They have made more progress in preserving business archives (e.g., the Business Archives Council) than North Americans have. The British Museum Library publishes guides to its manuscripts; local history associations publish parish records. There are also guides to diplomatic archives (see Daniel H. Thomas and Lynn M. Case, *Guide to the Diplomatic Archives of Western Europe* [Philadelphia: University of Pennsylvania, 1959]).

Many manuscripts are in private hands and may be traced through the catalogues and records of sale by commercial firms such as Sotheby's and Parke-Bernet or in the advertisements and brochures published by small antiquarian auctioneers. Rare books may also be found in this manner. Some research libraries preserve these catalogues, which are helpful in identifying various editions of a work and locating purchases of rare materials. Private collectors usually permit scholars to see the rare works in their collections.

Genealogy

A multitude of biographical dictionaries and directories, including the *New York Times* Obituaries volume, are part of genealogical research, although they are not usually found in the genealogical departments. Books and pamphlets on families by genealogists fill the shelves of NYPL's U.S. History, Local History and Genealogy Division, as do city directories, county and parish records, editions of Burke's *Peerage* and *Landed Gentry,* census records, and many others.

Once ensconced in the division, genealogical researchers rarely research outside it except for travelling to distant places to inspect local archives, courthouse records, and other genealogical collections. Occasionally you can avoid travelling. For instance, the mecca for genealogists is the Mormon Archives in Salt Lake City, Utah. Many genealogy divisions, like NYPL's, carry the *Mormon's International Genealogical Index,* the 1984 edition of which has 88 million names on microfiche. About 9 million names are added to the index every year. You look up a name under a major locality. When you find a reference to a parish register or other kind of record, you go to the Library of the Mormon Temple in your area of the country; for instance, in New York City it is on 65th Street and Broadway. Through it you can borrow the record on microfilm from the Archives in Salt Lake City. A useful guide is Timothy Beard's *How to Find Your Family Roots* (New York: McGraw-Hill, 1977).

This kind of research most closely approaches detective work, which calls for a basic scepticism. Genealogical research is complex; the few guides just skim the surface. To illustrate its complexities, let us look closely at U.S. censuses and passenger records.

U.S. Name Censuses. The name censuses taken in the United States every 10 years from 1790 (the first true census anywhere in the world) to 1930 are available on microfilm. (Information on names in later censuses may be obtained by writing to the Personal Census Records Office, Bureau of Census, Pittsburgh, Kansas.) The 1890 census of names was largely destroyed by a fire at the Department of Commerce in 1921. For the early censuses, only the names of the heads of households are given.

From 1790 to 1850 there are indexes by name for each state that direct you to the reel and page number of the national censuses. For the name censuses of 1860 and 1870, you can use city directories to find the residence of the individual, then use maps to determine the Assembly District or political division. The New York maps for 1860 give you the reel and page numbers directly; for New York in 1870 you must use the maps and then a guide that gives you the reel and page number. Other states have compiled similar maps as keys to the censuses found at their Genealogical Society Libraries.

For the 1880 name census for New York, several steps must be taken to find the reel and page number: (1) Check the name in the 1880–1 New York City residential directory for the home address. (2) In the same directory, in the attached city register section, check the street directory for the exact location of the address. (3) Locate the address on the enclosed assembly district maps (with the large numbers), noting also the election district (small black numbers). (4) Locate the corresponding assembly and election districts on the enclosed tables. Follow the line across to the enumeration district and finally to the reel number. (5) Fill out the call slip with the classmark, *ZI-50, and the reel number. (6) In the upper left-hand corner of each census schedule is the enumeration district. The schedules are arranged numerically by enumeration districts. Check the district schedule for the address of the person or family you seek. The desired information should be here, providing the subject resided at the given address at the time the census was taken – about June 1, 1880.

The 1900 names census has a Soundex approach, which is a system of coding surnames by number. (Libraries can provide you with the detailed instructions.) From the code you can find the reel and page numbers to the microfilm.

For the 1910 name census, you use the city directories to find the street address, then proceed to a guide indexed by street to find the election district. When you have the election district, the same guide gives you the reel and page numbers on the microfilm.

NYPL's U.S. History, Local History and Genealogy Division has a card index (by geographical area) to published censuses and local name surveys from colonial times to 1920. Federal law prohibits the release of census information until 72 years after its compilation.

The National Archives for the Northeastern United States at 201 Varick Street, New York City, contains 65,000 cubic feet of records from court records of the *Rosenberg* and *Hiss* cases; patent disputes involving Edison and Bell; Revolutionary War pension applications; limitation of liability suits involving the *Titanic*, the *Lusitania*, and the *Andrea Doria;* to the first *Batman* comic book. Census records are there too.

Passenger Lists. Passenger lists are on microfilm in the National Archives in Washington, DC. If you know the name of the vessel and approximate time of arrival and the port of arrival, you can find the passenger rather easily. Research libraries have many of these microfilms; for instance, NYPL has the *Register of Vessels Arriving at the Port of New York, 1789–1919,* in 27 reels arranged by date.

There are a number of indexes to these passenger lists, some specialized by ethnic group and others by time period. The following larger indexes are organized by surname:

U.S. National Archives:

- *Index to Passenger Lists of Vessels Arriving at New York, 1820–1846* (Washington, DC, 1958; 103 reels)
- *Index to Passenger Lists of Vessels Arriving at New York, June 16, 1897–June 30, 1902* (many reels)
- *Alphabetical Index to Passengers, 1906–1942* (in book volumes at the National Archives)

Some helpful guides are:

- P. William Filby (with Mary K. Meyer), *Passenger and Immigration Lists Index* (a guide to published arrival records of about

500,000 passengers who came to the United States and Canada
in the seventeenth, eighteenth, and nineteenth centuries;
Detroit: Gale, 1981; annual supplements)
* *Passenger and Immigration Lists Bibliography, 1538–1900* (a guide
to published works of arrivals in the United States and Canada;
Detroit: Gale, 1981)

Special collections may be devoted to special subjects – for
example, the NYPL's Jewish Division covering religion, history,
culture, and current events; its Arents Collections devoted solely
to works about tobacco and 'books in part'; its Dance Collection;
and its Map Division. These have special bibliographies and
guides.

Newspapers

Old newspapers are invaluable sources for researchers, for obituaries and, most important, for a social and economic picture of
the past. Most are kept on microfilm and are readily obtained
through interlibrary loan if your research library does not have
them. The indexes to newspapers are informative in themselves;
for instance, the famous case of the Quinn papers in the New
York Public Library in the mid-1960s was indexed in the *New York
Times* as shown in Figure 4.1.

Patents

Much of patents research is computerized today. Patent diagrams
can be brought to the monitor screen. Patent specifications,
abstracts of patents, patents lists, and related periodicals and
books are what you work with to find if an invention has been pat-
ented. The NYPL Patents Collection, for instance, receives publications on patents from the United States, England, France,
Germany, and about 35 other countries. It has a comprehensive
historical collection as well. The two major publications you will
use are U.S. Patent Office, *Index of Patents* (1790–) and *Manual of
Classification.*

Fig. 4.1

QUINN, John (1869-1924)

P Kavanagh pub on home-made press vol of excerpts from Quinn's literary lrs by memorizing them after readings in NY Pub Library; Quinn's will gave lrs to Library on condition they be read by scholars but not copied or pub till '88; Kavanagh comments, Ja 17,1:3; ct, at Library request, orders Kavanagh to show cause why books should not be destroyed; Library dir Freehafer comments, Ja 21, 28:6; ed, Ja 22,26:2; lr, Ja 25,26:5; Kavanagh cuts books in half, gives ct half; gets permission to keep 2 copies; has sent copy to Brit Museum and gave 9 copies to P Farrell; Farrell refuses to give them up; will fight any action by Library, Ja 26,1:2

NYC Sheriff, under NY Pub Library writ, searches P Farrell apt for 9 of Kavanagh's home-made books; friend of Farrell takes books out during search; Library withdraws writ, F 24,39:4

Trademark publications can be found for all countries represented by patents. The New York Public Library has a catalogue of trademarks registered in the U.S. Patent Office through part of 1947, which has been superseded by *Trademark Register* (1961–4, 1967–) and *Trademark Renewal Register* (1964 and 1966). For other special catalogues and files on patents and trademarks, see page 288 of *Guide to the Research Collections of The New York Public Library* (Chicago: ALA, 1975) compiled by Sam P. Williams.

Picture Collections

The Picture Collection at NYPL's Mid-Manhattan Library is used largely by commercial artists who borrow pictures for aid in their artwork and design. For readers seeking illustrations to accompany a book or article, the most important thing to remember is to ask the librarian for the subject, such as 'I want a picture of a printing press,' not 'I want a picture of the process of printing.'

The collection has 15,000 subject headings. Culled from books, magazines, newspapers, and other sources, each mounted picture is given a number by which you can look up a bibliographic citation of the publication from which it came. The source catalogue holds 19,000 citations.

The collection is divided at the year 1906. Pictures after 1906 are kept by subject heading in vertical files as the main part of the collection. Here, readers may borrow pictures for reproduction purposes or to use in design and artwork (other libraries will photocopy such material). Pictures before that date are kept in vertical files in a special area; they are not loaned, but may be photocopied.

Special collections of postcards depicting places; an alphabetical file of royalty, by country; a personalities file, by name; and a geographic clipping file are also included in the Picture Collection.

The following are some bibliographic sources for picture collections:

- Jessie Croft Ellis, *Index to Illustrations* (Boston: Faxon, 1966)
- Isabel Stevenson Munro and Kate M. Munro, *Index to Reproductions of European Paintings* (New York: H.W. Wilson, 1956)
- Jessie Croft Ellis, *Nature and Its Applications* (over 200,000 selected references to nature forms and illustrations of nature, as used in every way; Boston: Faxon, 1949)
- *Illustration Index* (Metuchen, NJ: Scarecrow Press, 1957) plus additional compilations covering 1950 to the present.
- Jane Clapp, *Art in Life* (New York: Scarecrow Press, 1959) and Supplement (1965)

Copyright. When you republish pictures, you should be careful to get permission from whoever holds the copyright. According to copyright law, items published with notice of copyright before 1978 are copyrighted for 28 years and can be renewed for another 28 years. For photos published after 1978, the copyright duration is for the author's lifetime plus 50 years. For works made for hire, copyright lasts for 75 years from the date of publication, or 100 years from its creation, whichever is less. Copyrights made before 1978 but renewed after 1978 are renewable for 47 years.

In this regard the Picture Collection's sources file, to which each picture is linked by its unique number, is particularly useful. Often, of course, for pictures from old periodicals and books with no available current address of publisher, permission to publish can be safely disregarded – not, however, for still-flourishing magazines like the *New Yorker.*

Since copyright laws vary by country, you should check *Copyright Laws and Treaties of the World* (Paris: UNESCO), which is kept current by supplements in every major library.

RESEARCHING IN THE PERFORMING ARTS

Theatre

You begin your research by thinking of the type of materials you will be looking at – published works, playscripts, prompt books, clippings, old newspapers, periodicals, playbills, programs, photographs, letters, documents. These are all found in a great collection such as NYPL's Billy Rose Theatre Collection. You may find yourself jumping from one type of material to another as you compare prompt books with playscripts, reviews in the clipping file with comments in published memoirs, or photographs of the stage with movie stills (the NYPL collection has 2 million glossy movie stills). Much of this material is found by author or subject in the collection's special card catalogue.

You will have to consult other library departments because the collections overlap. For instance, typed librettos of musical comedies are kept in the Billy Rose Theatre Collection but the published librettos are in the Music Division. On the other hand, both published and typed filmscripts are in the Theatre Collection. The Berg Collection has letters and scripts of dramatists and actors. Check the other great theatre collections: the Harvard and Yale University Libraries, the Players Club on Gramercy Park, New York City, and the Schubert Archives of New York City. New York University's Tamiment Library has the Archives of Actor's Equity, the American Guild of Variety Artists, and other groups.

Photographs

To find who holds the copyright on photographs, you can use *The Theater World*, an annual pictorial history for the season. (*Screen World* and *Dance World* are helpful resources as well.) The *New York Times* is a good source, because it includes the name of the photographer under the photograph.

Theatre Database

The Theater Research Data Center at Brooklyn College, in New York City, built a data bank of articles, books, theses, films, microfilm, folios – every form of published material on the subject of theatre. It is international in scope, with input at present from 14 nations and document centres in Europe and Asia. It may be accessed through the online network system of City University of New York (CUNY). The entries are arranged according to the five major classification headings for theatre, and the standard subject headings for theatre are used. The system includes a subject index, a document author index, and a content index arranged by geographic location. An annual printed bibliography lists the inputs during the year, beginning with *International Bibliography of the Theater: 1982* (Brooklyn: Theater Research Data Center, 1985).

Theatre Sources

- Marion K. Whalan, *Performing Arts Research* (a guide to information sources; Detroit: Gale, 1976). This is one of several bibliographies to all aspects and types of materials in the performing arts information guide series issued by the publisher Gale.
- *Performing Arts Libraries and Museums of the World,* 3rd ed. (Paris: Centre National de la Recherche Scientifique, 1984).

Music

A large portion of music research parts company with the usual sort of research in published and unpublished sources – that is, the study of musical scores to establish either the composer or the latest and best score. This is meticulous work that requires gathering of bits of information from manuscript sources, scores, and contemporary accounts, often over the course of a researcher's lifetime before a pattern is found.

An international joint effort has been made to control information on music written before 1800, with the RISM (Répertoire International des Sources Musicales/International Inventory of Musical Sources) *Einzeldrucke vor 1800* (Kassel: Barenreiter; London: Basel Tours), published in a multivolume set.

RISM is establishing a data bank for musical manuscripts before 1800. The system will have an added advantage: the musical beginnings to pieces can be fed into the data bank, which facilitates identification.

A major difficulty with using catalogues to music collections is the variety of ways in which scores are catalogued. In the United States, alone, the conventional title is used.

The great music collections are in the Oesterreichisches Nationalbibliothek and the Gesellschaft für Musikfreunde in Vienna. Italy has several good libraries. (See RISM's *Directory of Music Research Libraries*: vol. 1, Canada and the United States; vol. 2, Thirteen European countries; vol. 3, Spain, France, Italy, Portugal; vol. 4, Australia, Israel, Japan, New Zealand.)

Bibliographic Sources

- Vincent Druckles, *Music Reference and Research Materials*, 3rd ed. (New York: Free Press, 1974)
- Ruth T. Watanabe, *Introduction to Music Research* (Englewood Cliffs, NJ: Prentice-Hall, 1967)
- Anna Harriett Heyer, *Historical Sets, Collected Editions, and Monuments of Music* (a guide to their contents), 3rd ed. (Chicago: ALA, 1980) in 2 vols. (It lists the publications and gives bibliographic information and list of contents.)
- *Music Index* (Harmonic Park Press)
- *International Index to Music Periodicals* (Chadwyck-Healey)

Dance

To approach a unique collection in a research library, you should read the description of its resources in the library's *Guide* before using the collection. In the case of the NYPL's Dance Collection at the Performing Arts Research Center, for example, you should read the detailed description in the *Guide to the Research Collections of the New York Public Library,* compiled by Sam Williams (Chicago: ALA, 1975, 150–6). It tells you that the Dance Collection includes ethnic, primitive, folk and modern dance, ballet, and social forms as various as the minuet and cha-cha; that pictorial material forms the major part of the collection; and that it has tens of thousands of prints, librettos, stage designs, programs, and other material and thousands of reels of motion picture film. The library's most recently published brochures and reports will provide the latest information. Readers at the collection are often dancers seeking to re-create dances from still photographs, as Nureyev re-created Nijinsky's 'The Afternoon of a Faun' (1912) from the Library's collection of Nijinsky photographs.

The *Dance Collection Dictionary Catalog,* therefore, is an amalgam of special files organized by dance steps, titles of dances, dance iconography, and other systems, and the regular book-catalogue form of entry. The entries are arranged under established headings of the form of the material: books and periodical articles, visual material, music, and audio material. You will find that the scope is broad; for instance, entries for individual titles cover professional performances and note the first performance, the first performance in the United States, the first performance in New York, the first performance by a major company other than the original, and also performances with new or revised staging or choreography.

MEDICAL LIBRARIES

You cannot afford to overlook other specialized libraries in doing research. For instance, the great collection of the New York Academy of Medicine Library (2 East 103 Street, New York City) is open to the public. Here you can find almost every publication on medicine and related subjects such as psychoanalysis, pharmacy, foods, and cookery. The library collects rare books and incunabula on medicine, minutes of medical societies, portraits of medical men, and many other materials. It collects all editions of medical works in all languages. Having all editions in all languages is important to the researcher; for example, William Harvey wrote in Latin, but translations of his works include commentaries and additional material. The library currently receives 4,000 serial titles and has a great collection of old medical periodicals in all languages.

You can find reports on the diseases of well-known and unknown people, correspondence of medical men from all over the world, from modern to ancient times, a portrait catalogue of medical people, and a catalogue of illustrations analysed by the librarians from publications on the history of medicine. These sources are useful for researchers in other fields. Those who picture medical libraries as containing mainly indexes and abstracts of medical articles, much of it online, will be surprised to learn that the library collects works of history comprehensively, because medicine must be studied in relation to the world around it.

LAW

To begin research in U.S. law, you should turn first to *Shepard's Citations,* to determine the current status of your primary legal source (i.e., a decision, statute, or an administrative regulation or ruling). This research step is essential because of the doctrine of precedent and *stare decisis,* and because, strictly speaking, decisions and statutes remain in effect, regardless of their age, unless and until they are reversed, overruled, or, in the case of statutes, repealed or judicially declared void.

Shepard's citator system comprises state units, regional units, federal units, and specialized citator units. Many nations have equivalent citator systems.

Major research libraries carry the laws of all nations and of all state or regional units. You can differentiate between slip laws and consolidated laws or revised statutes. Slip laws are the laws issued by a legislature during the year and are bound together in order of issue. To find a slip law, you must know the year it was passed. Consolidated laws are the laws in force, brought together in a uniform set of volumes with indexes. In earlier years they were called revised statutes. You can also use these consolidated laws to find laws that are no longer in force, because under the wording of the law or statute there is a list of citations of the laws from which it was derived. You then find the earlier law by year in the slip laws. For instance, the *United States Code* may refer to a historical precedent as 12Stat. 146. This earlier law is found in *The United States Statutes*, vol. 12, p. 146.

If you are preparing your own case, you should be familiar with the volumes of *Federal Procedure* (Rochester, NY: Lawyers Cooperative Publishing Co.), which is arranged alphabetically and explains the procedure for bringing your case to federal criminal and civil courts and administrative boards. Along with these volumes, you need *Federal Procedural Forms*, by the same publisher.

The best access to case law, by subject, is *West's Federal Practice Digests*. There are four editions, each covering a different time period.

Finally, law libraries keep sample briefs on file, useful for someone who needs a model to prepare a brief on a certain subject for a certain court.

Law libraries are open to the public in some countries such as England. In the United States they are usually private. In New York City, however, the U.S. Court of Appeals Library on the 25th floor of the U.S. Courthouse, Foley Square, admits public researchers, although technically it is for the court staff. The New York Public Library issues METRO cards to readers to visit university law libraries in the New York City area for legal publications that the public library does not carry.

GENERAL RULES FOR WHEN TO USE WHAT

1. When doing research on a general topic, break it down into

smaller topics, which you can then relate better to the reference guides, the catalogue subject entries, and bibliographies.

2. For historical research, begin by looking under subject headings in the library catalogues.

3. For current research, begin by looking in the periodical indexes in your subject field.

4. When researching a project for a long period, vary your search from events to biographies to theory, to avoid becoming stale. This also gives you fresh ideas by showing you former sources in the light of a new approach.

5. Research, by its nature, requires you to redefine your goals at intervals. This must be done at the right times; otherwise, you waste your time and, perhaps, lose your way.

6. Research tools, such as online information systems, which are subsidiary to the catalogue, must be regarded as mere helpmeets. The library catalogue and accompanying indexes to the collection not in the catalogue are your fundamental tools. You work with the collection and get your inspiration and pleasure from it. Online systems and periodical indexes are patterned by others, but your research must be unique as you develop your own pattern.

7. Remember the variety of forms in which you may find your material. Special pamphlet collections, manuscript collections, and photograph and print collections may help you pursue your subject. Always keep an eye peeled for book catalogues to these special collections.

8. Remember the *National Union Catalog of Books and Pamphlets*, the *Union List of Serials*, and other bibliographic location guides. Extend the walls of your research library to encompass the North American continent through the services of the interlibrary loan.

9. Researchers in the humanities should rely first on book bibliographies; in the social sciences and the sciences, you should rely first on periodical indexes and abstracts.

10. Always use the same notebooks in your research. Scraps of paper and occasional notebooks will most likely be lost. Also, it helps to keep a record near you of what you have seen.

Many researchers have begun to study the same book twice. And keep a full bibliographical record of your sources, and that means page numbers as well. Trying to relocate a source can be mental torture.

WHEN TO USE OTHER LIBRARIES

Avoid beginning research in a small library; you will just be discouraged prematurely. Pack up and go to Washington, New York, Paris, or London. If you use a major university library, the resources of the large research libraries will be available to you through interlibrary loan.

If you are researching in medicine, you must use a medical library because general research libraries do not collect in the field. In the United States, researchers in law can find fundamental legal information – law, cases, forms guides, and legal periodicals (for which they use the *Index to Legal Periodicals*) – but study beyond the superficial requires permission to use one of the private law libraries, which can be difficult to obtain.

If researching in a specialized subject, you should go directly to the collection that appears to have the most material; for instance, when studying the American Revolutionary War in New York State, you would research in the manuscript collections in the New York Historical Society; later you would visit the New York State Library in Albany and the American Antiquarian Society in Worcester, Massachusetts. The New York Public Library also has strong early American collections. First, of course, you would have read the major published works on the subject, which you should be able to obtain in a medium-sized city library. Once a general understanding is formed, a deeper knowledge can be obtained only by studying the primary materials. At this point, your research begins.

THE MICROFORM PROBLEM – HOW TO DEAL WITH IT

The polluted air and acidic paper of the industrialized era have turned library materials to sawdust. A rescue operation called 'conservation' treated old paper with chemicals to hold it together until it could be microfilmed. Libraries pooled their resources and funds in microform projects such as the National Gazettes on Microform, which involved libraries internationally.

Aside from the necessity of preservation, library administrators became worried about shelf space. They saw microform as an answer to space problems. They began buying microfilm runs of periodical sets and throwing out the bound copies, regardless of the perfect state of the paper. Current periodicals were no longer bound, but purchased in microfilm reels. Government publications, particularly the all-important U.S. congressional hearings, were purchased on microfiches; indexes to them were purchased from the same company, thus obviating the need to enter them into the library catalogue. The administrators explained that this saved money in bindery expenses and cataloguing time.

Because administrators are not researchers, they could not have understood the difficulty of locating materials, especially congressional hearings, in the library catalogues. This difficulty is increased when items in the collection are not catalogued; indeed, it throws the researcher on the mercy of the librarian for information on where such items may be found and for guidance through the intricate procedure of locating the microfiche copy.

Also, administrators are not aware of the impracticality of researching with microform when indexes (which are somewhere else on the reel or on another fiche) have to be constantly consulted, necessitating frequent changing of reels or fiche on the reading machine. With frequent use, microform becomes scratched, sometimes illegible. Although desperate attempts are being made to improve microform readers, they cause great discomfort to the reader compelled to sit at them for any length of time. Regarding storage, it can fit into a smaller space than a book, but it can be lost or stolen more easily. And if it has not been catalogued, its loss will not be known unless some attempt is made to record its presence in the library's collection.

Not being researchers, library administrators also have no idea of the eye strain experienced by researchers when reading microform. But because 'the microform solution' (with its accompanying expense to libraries and bonanza to microform companies) has been widely adopted, researchers must look to their own defences.

The use of microfilm for spot references can be helpful in research libraries, as the films are made available quickly and modern machines can roll the film speedily, thus avoiding the tiresome cranking of the old reading machines. But for reading at length, the researcher should avoid the microforms if possible. Here are some tips on how this can be done:

1. For very important papers, research libraries may keep two copies: one on microform and one in paper. The microform is given to students and casual researchers. For those reading at length in these papers, the paper copy can be located. The New York Public Library Research Libraries, for example, make the U.S. congressional set of reports and documents available in microprint cards, but also preserve the bound volumes. Of great value is the original bound collection of Great Britain Parliamentary Papers (Great Britain. Parliament. *Sessional Papers*). (An Irish reprint edition lacks some of the important papers.) Foolishly, some libraries discarded their bound volumes for microprint and microfiche copies, which researchers hate to use not only because of the eye strain but because they make browsing through them impossible.
2. There may be libraries in the same city that still keep on paper the pamphlets and periodicals that your major research library has converted to microform. You can either arrange to use that library or ask for the materials through interlibrary loan.
3. If the volumes can be found only in microform, the reader can have them photocopied (at a high cost) and take them home to read. The clearinghouse for *Dissertations Abstracts* in Ann Arbor, Michigan, provides researchers with either microfilm or xerox volume of the dissertation requested.
4. If back issues of periodicals are on microfilm, the reader may procure back issues in paper from the publisher.

Admittedly, these strategies cause delay and inconvenience, but researchers may wish to adopt them to save themselves from eye strain.

Appendix

World's Major Research Libraries and Methods of Approach

This appendix contains brief summaries of some of the world's major research libraries and the different methods of searching required in each. It is always advisable to confirm hours and location of any special divisions before you visit.

THE NEW YORK PUBLIC LIBRARY

Central Research Library

Central Building
42nd St. and Fifth Ave., New York, NY, 10018
Hours: Main Reading Room: Mon., Thurs., Fri., Sat. Open: 10 A.M.–6 P.M., Tues., Wed. 11 A.M.–7:30 P.M. Other divisions have different hours. The 43rd Street Annex off Tenth Avenue is open 9 A.M.–4:45 P.M., Mon.–Sat.

Admission. No card or admission ticket is required, except for the Special Collections, for which you can obtain a pass from the Special Collections Admissions Office.

Layout. The New York Public Library provides a good example of how research libraries are divided into subject divisions. All libraries have a central catalogue room and central reading room. Special divisions are in the same building or other buildings either in the next block or miles away. Sometimes the special divisions have direct communication with the central reading room by which you can request books from the special divisions to read in the central reading room. In other cases, the special divisions are completely separated from the central reading room, and you must go to those divisions to read their books. The NYPL Web site has floor plans, which you should check because the library is going through a reorganization of its special divisions as this book goes to press.

The front entrance to NYPL's Central Research Library is from Fifth Avenue. Exhibit halls encompass the central portion of the ground floor. Down the hallway to your left is the Periodicals Section (Room 108), where you can read current periodicals in the humanities and those of a general nature. ('Current' means periodicals issued within the present year.) If you continue to your left, you will pass along a hallway leading to the Microform Section (Room 100), which has over 320,000 microfiches and microfilms of historical files of newspapers, periodicals, pamphlets, and large literary sets. (Some microforms you can find only in the subject divisions). Retracing your steps and moving down the hallway to the north, you find the Local History and Genealogy Division (Room 121), where the histories of counties, cities, and smaller incorporations are kept with the genealogical publications (the histories of nations are located in the General Research Division.) Across the hallway is the Map Division (Room 119).

On this right side of the building is an elevator, as well as a marble stairway; stairs also lead from either side of the front foyer. Taking the elevator to the second floor, you will find the Scholars' Center (Room 228), which includes the former Wertheim Study and Allen Room for researchers and writers using the Library's collection. Proceeding down the second-floor hallway, you will find a central corridor branching off at a right angle. Down this corridor is the Slavonic Division (Room 217) for literature, including periodicals, in the Slavonic languages, and the Oriental Division (Room 219) for literature, including periodicals, in the Oriental languages. At the far end of the main hallway are the Administrative Offices of the Library and the Research Libraries.

Proceeding up the stairway to the third floor, you will encounter, leading off from the centre of the hallway, the General Research Division (Room 315), where the central catalogue room is located; beyond this is the two-part central or Main Reading Room. In Room 315 the computer and book catalogues for all the works in the Research Libraries are kept, including those of the special divisions. Internet stations are kept here for readers to use for 15 minutes or less. Here, also, are research librarians ready to help you locate materials and file request slips for publications.

Beyond this outer room, two reading halls, divided by an enclosure, provide you with many reading tables and ready reference books lining the shelves. At the centre enclosure are light indicators that display numbers when requested books are brought up from the book stacks below.

In the reading room to the right (the North Hall, as distinct from the reading room on the left, which is called the South Hall) is an area of workstations for consulting CD-ROMs of indexes, full-text journal articles, encyclopedias, and world library catalogues as well as more Internet workstations. At the end of the North Hall you will find the Rare Books and Manuscripts Division. The South Hall Reading Room has a Multimedia Center where you can view videotapes and use digitally formatted materials stored in the library stacks. Resources containing audio or video, and certain materials listed in CATNYP (the online catalogue) under the call numbers *WG, *B, and *U are available for use at these workstations by appointment only. There is seating for 636 readers in the North and South Halls. At the end of the South Hall is the Art and Architecture Division. The Art Room for researchers in the fine arts is open without restriction, but the Print and Photographic Collections off the third-floor hallway (Rooms 313 and 308) require a special reader's pass from the Special Collections Office (Room 316).

On the north side in the third-floor hallway is the Pforzheimer Collection, 'Shelley and His Circle,' devoted to works of the English Romantic poets (Room 319) and, across the hall from it, the Berg Collection of rare books and manuscripts in English and American literature. Around the bend in the hallway is the Arents

Collection of works on tobacco and books in parts (Room 324). All of these collections require the special reader's pass.

Taking the elevator down to the ground floor, you will come across the Jewish Division (Room 84) near the 42nd Street entrance. The Jewish Division has materials relating to Jewish culture and religion, including periodicals and publications in microform. Directly opposite the 42nd Street entrance is the Celeste Bartos Forum, where the library hosts talks by distinguished speakers.

Science, Industry and Business Library

At 188 Madison Avenue, between 34th and 35th Streets, about a 10-minute walk from the Central Building, the Library's science and business books and periodicals are kept. (These do not include books and periodicals of the social sciences, which are in the Central Building.) The Research Collection of 500 seats for readers is on the lower level, and a circulating collection is on the street level. The Research Collection also contains newspapers and periodicals on microfilm, government publications, many of which are on microform, and a complete file of United States patents and a premier collection of foreign patents. (The NYPL's former Newspaper Division and Patents and Trademarks Collection were incorporated into the Business Library.) There is an open-shelf reference collection of 60,000 volumes. On the lower level as well is the Electronic Information Center with 70 computer workstations and printers offering access to more than 100 stand-alone CD-ROM databases, networked CD-ROM files, online full-text electronic journals, the Internet, including the World Wide Web, and other electronic resources covering the latest in science, business, and government information. Training classes in the use of electronic methods of research are provided to the public in the Center.

Performing Arts Research Center

To reach the Music Division, the Billy Rose Theatre Collection, the Rodgers and Hammerstein Archives of Recorded Sound, and the Dance Collection from the Central Building, you take a 104 bus on the opposite side of 42nd St. going west for about 20 minutes to the Lincoln Center complex at Broadway and 65th Street. Between the Opera House and the Vivian Beaumont Theater is an entrance to the Library & Museum of the Performing Arts. On the first two floors are the Branch Libraries units. On the third floor are the above-mentioned collections of the NYPL Research Libraries' Performing Arts Research Center.

Schomburg Center for Research in Black Culture

This collection of publications and manuscripts related to black culture is housed in a modern research library building at 135th Street. On leaving the central building, you would go to the Times Square subway station and take the uptown No. 2 train of the IRT Seventh Avenue express line. This takes you directly to the Schomburg Center at the 135th Street stop.

The center comprises several sections, each dedicated to the acquisition of the format of materials it represents such as General Research and Reference, Rare Books, Manuscripts and Archives, Moving Images and Recorded Sound, Arts and Artifacts, Photographs and Prints, and so on.

Items in the NYPL catalogues with call numbers beginning with 'Sc' are in the Schomburg Center.

Annex

Publications that have been crowded out of the central building are kept in the Annex; for instance, books on religion are shelved here. To visit the Annex, you take a 105 bus across the street from the 42nd Street entrance of the Central Building, going west for about 10 minutes to Tenth Avenue on 42nd Street, and walk one block north to West 43rd Street and then west for a quarter-block to the New York Public Library Annex at 521 West 43rd Street. The Library also stores books in a shared offsite facility near Princeton, New Jersey.

Connections with the Main Reading Room

Rather than travel to the Annex to read a book, you may request it through the Information Desk in Room 315. The requested book will arrive in two days and be put under your name on the reserve shelves, where it will remain for a week.

Publications in all other special divisions you must request and read in those divisions. Note carefully the hours when the special divisions are open because they may differ from the hours of the Main Reading Room and from each other.

Mid-Manhattan Library

The Mid-Manhattan Library is the main library of the NYPL Branch Libraries. Located on Fifth Avenue and 40th Street across from the Central Research Library, it has both circulating and reference books. For periodicals and books that the Research Libraries do not have, you should check in the book and online Catalogues of the Branch Libraries to see if they are available for you to borrow or read at the Mid-Manhattan Library or at other branches. If periodicals you want are in use at The Research Libraries, you may find them at Mid-Manhattan. The Research Libraries, for example, do not collect books on medicine, but the Science Department in the circulating collection in the Science, Industry and Business Library does keep such books. This circulating Science Collection and the circulating Economics and Business Section are found on the ground floor of the Science, Industry and Business Library on Madison Avenue and 34th Street.

The Andrew Heiskell Library for the Blind and Physically Handicapped of the New York Public Library, at 40 West 20th Street, is part of the Branch Libraries system.

HARVARD UNIVERSITY LIBRARY

Harvard University, Cambridge, MA, 02138 (branches in other locations, e.g., Boston; Washington, DC; Florence, Italy). Tel.:

(617) 495–1000. For hours and catalogue information, check the university's home page (http://hul.harvard.edu/).

Background. Founded in 1638, it is the oldest library in the United States and the largest university library in the world.

Admission. If you are not from Harvard, write to the librarian to obtain permission to use the library. Harry Elkins Widener Memorial Library, Harvard Yard, Cambridge, MA, 02138. Tel.: (617) 495–2411.

Layout. The library consists of more than 10 million volumes and more than 90 libraries, many of which service the particular professional school to which they are attached; thus, they tend to be subject-specialty libraries – for business, law, medicine, education, or divinity, for example. Others are truly specialized libraries – those for the arts; music; rare books and manuscripts; the physical, applied, and biological sciences, among others. Also within these libraries are specialized collections. The main research library is the Widener Library in the centre of the campus; it serves the social sciences and humanities. The visitor should seek information on the research collections at Harvard from the numerous publications available and from the Widener reference staff. Most Harvard libraries allow university-affiliated users to borrow materials. As in most university libraries, the reader can retrieve his or her books directly from the stacks.

Catalogues. Every Harvard Library or specialized collection has its own catalogue. The Union Catalog, a card catalogue by author that was closed off in 1977, is located on the main floor of the Widener Library and contains the majority of Harvard's earlier holdings. For the period from 1977 to date, you can use the Distributable Union Catalog (DUC) in microfiche, which covers most of the Harvard libraries and can be found in 130 locations. It is divided into an author-title section, a subject section, a medical subject section, and a monthly author-title supplement. Not listed in the DUC, but found in individual library catalogues, are works in Arabic, Chinese, Japanese, Korean, other languages of East Asia, older books in Hebrew and Yiddish, manuscripts, archival materials, maps, sound recordings, and visual materials.

Hollis is Harvard's online catalogue of the holdings of all Harvard University libraries and related databases. Other Harvard University library databases may be found at www.harvard.edu/museums.

BRITISH LIBRARY (ENGLAND)

Reference Division St. Pancras, 96 Euston Road, London NW1 2DB. (Tel: 44 171 412 7677; Fax: 44 171 412 7794). Hours: Mon., Wed., Thurs., Fri, 9:30 A.M.–6 P.M.; Tues., 9:30 A.M.–8 P.M.; Sat. 9:30 A.M.–5 P.M.; Sun. 11 A.M.–5 P.M. Closed for the week following the last complete week in October, and on major holidays.

Background. The library's nucleus consists of the collection of books and manuscripts brought together on the foundation of the British Museum in 1753. The old Royal Library was given to the British Museum in 1757, and the right to a deposit copy of every book published in the United Kingdom was transferred with it. Foreign material is obtained by purchase or exchange from most countries. The total number of books exceeds 10 million.

Admission. Free, but you must obtain a reader's ticket with a letter of reference from a professor or consulate official.

Layout. The Department of Printed Books or the Humanities Reading Room on the ground floor consists of the central reading halls and contains books and periodicals on all subjects. In addition, at the Euston St. building are the Oriental and India Office Collections, the Science Reference and Information Service, the Rare Books and Music Reading Room, the Manuscripts Reading Room, the National Sound Archive, the Philatelic Collection, the Map Collection, and the Patent Collection. Here also is the Social Policy Information Service, housing the largest collection in Europe of official papers of all periods, including government and intergovernment publications.

The Newspaper Library at Colindale, North London, contains newspapers published after 1800, from all countries, and British provincial papers published before 1800.

The library also has photo reproduction facilities.

Catalogues. The General Catalogue is contained in looseleaf volumes shelved at the centre of the Reading Room. It contains entries for works received in the Department of Printed Books through 1970, which are arranged in columns by main entry, with supplementary slips for works added to the collections from 1956 to 1970 and mounted beside the columns from 1975. A published Subject Index to the General Catalogue covers accessions from 1861 to 1960, in book form, with acquisitions from 1961 in microform cassettes. Blaise, the British Library's online bibliographic service, covers materials accessed from 1970. For the other departments you should use the catalogues particular to them. They are listed on the British Library's home page on the Internet (http://portico.bl.uk/).

Requesting Books. When you fill out call slips and leave them at the central desk, the books are brought to the seat number you have written on the call slip. Delivery can take more than an hour. You must return your books to the central desk and retrieve your request slip.

To avoid waiting for books to be delivered, you may post request slips to the library up to 24 hours in advance. The books are kept on reserve for you.

Useful Guides:

Janet Foster and Julia Sheppard, *British Archives: A Guide to Archive Resources in the United Kingdom* (Detroit: Gale, 1982)
Maurice F. Bond, *Guide to the Records of Parliament* (London: HMSO: 1971)

Jane Cox and Timothy Padfield, *Tracing Your Ancestors in the Public Record Office* (London: HMSO, 1983)

BIBLIOTHÈQUE NATIONALE (FRANCE)

58 rue Richelieu, 75084 Paris Cedex 02 (Tel: 261-82-83)
Hours: Mon.–Sat., 9 A.M.–6P.M. Closed second and third weeks after Easter.

Background. The Bibliothèque du Roi began in the age of Charlemagne. It was housed first in the Louvre by Charles V, was broken up and reestablished at Fontainebleau in 1544, became a *dépôt légal*, was rehoused in the rue Vivienne in the age of Louis XIV, and grew rapidly in its present location until the Revolution. The new National Assembly then transformed it by requiring that it absorb all Parisian ecclesiastical libraries and aristocratic *émigré* libraries; by 1794 it had grown fivefold in five years.

Admission. You need a letter from a university official or your cultural attaché certifying your need to use the library. You pay a fee for an identification card and provide two full-face photographs, one of which is attached to your card.

Layout. The Central Reading Room, on the ground floor, contains books and publications for general research. Specialized departments in the building are maps and plans; stamps and photographs; manuscripts; coins, medals, and antiques; music; national record library and audiovisual aids; and theatre arts. Attached to it are the Bibliothèque de l'Arsenal (1 rue de Sully, 75004 Paris), specializing in literature and theatre, the Bibliothèque du Conservatoire, Nationale Supérieure de Musique (114 rue de Madrid, 75008 Paris), and the Bibliothèque-Musée de l'Opéra (Place Charles Garnier, 75009 Paris). In the central building the catalogue room (salle des catalogues) is reached from the Central Reading Room down a flight of stairs. It is a large room with a smaller adjoining periodicals room, where reference librarians are stationed.

Catalogues. The *Catalogue général des livres imprimés* contains more than 200 volumes arranged by author from A (published in 1897) through V (published in 1969). The date on which each volume was printed is on the cover, so that you know you cannot expect to find a publication published after that date in that volume. In this case, you turn to four other catalogues:

1. If the work is by an author whose name falls between VIB and Z, and was published before 1882, consult the card catalogue by authors of acquisitions prior to 1882.
2. If the work was acquired between 1882 and 1935, but too late to be included in the proper volume in the *Catalogue général*, it can be found in the sheaf catalogues with red and white backs.
3. If the work was received between 1936 and 1959, it can be found in the card catalogue of acquisitions between 1936 and 1959; if received between 1960 and 1969, it can be found in the card catalogue of acquisitions 1960–9; if received between 1970 and the present date, it can be found in the card catalogue for acquisitions since 1970.
4. Works between 1960 and 1964 can be found in the book *Catalogue général, auteurs et anonymes*, and in the card catalogue 1960–9. For anonymous or corporate authorship (public or private), look in the *Catalogue général, auteurs et anonymes* or in the special card catalogues for acquisitions from 1950 and 1960 to 1969 and 1970 plus.

Subject catalogues include the following:

1. 1882–94 in bound indexes.
2. 1894–1925 collections in mobile bindings with white and green backs.
3. 1925–35 collections bound in black cloth.
4. 1935–59 in card catalogues.
5. Since 1960 in card catalogues, or for the period 1960–4, in the *Catalogue général.*
6. BN-OPALE, the online catalogue, covers books accessioned since 1970 and periodicals after 1960.

7. BN-OPALE PLUS makes the books and periodicals available online searchable through the Internet. For a full description of these catalogues, check the library's homepage (http://www.bnf.fr/).

For recent books, when you know the year of publication, look in the *Bibliographie de la France*, which gives the Bibliothèque Nationale call number with the bibliographic description.

Requesting Books. You fill out a request slip with your seat number and hand it in to the library clerk in the central reading room. The books are delivered to your seat. Ten thousand reference works are available on the open shelves of the reading room, and a card index to them is located at the entrance.

Useful Guides:

France, Ministère de l'éducation nationale, *Catalogue général des manuscrits des bibliothèques publiques de France* (Paris: 1885–1965), 55 vols in 62
Librairies and Archives in France: A Handbook, edited by Erwin K. Welsch (Pittsburgh: Council for European Studies, 1973)

STATE V.I. LENIN LIBRARY OF THE RUSSIAN FEDERATION

101000 Moscow, Prospekt Kalinina, 3 (Tel: 202–57–90)
Hours: 9 A.M.–10 P.M. every day, including Sun. Closed on major holidays.

Background. Founded in 1862 as Rumyantsev Library and reorganized in 1925, the library now has more than 28 million books, periodicals, and serials, and complete files of newspapers in all 91 national languages and 156 foreign languages.

Admission. The library can be used only by students pursuing advanced degrees or by university-trained researchers. (Workers use the public libraries.) To obtain a reader's ticket, you should have an official letter verifying the purpose of your research, your passport, and photographs of yourself. You must go to the main reading room on the second floor of the new building.

Layout. All of the departments are contained in the same complex of the old building and the new building adjoining it. There are 22 reading rooms with 2,230 seats. The main reading halls in both buildings are found on the second floor. There is an annex in Khimki.

Catalogues. Each reading room covers a special subject and has its unique catalogue. The main catalogue room is on the second floor of the new building. There are 22 different catalogues for books, most of them alphabetical author catalogues, but some classified by subject or by geographic location. There are separate catalogues for periodicals, newspapers, books, and dissertations, and catalogues organized by languages (one alphabetical catalogue of Russian-language books, one for Ukrainian books, one for books in the Latin alphabet, one for books in the languages of the people's democracies of Asia). Subject catalogues for scientific disciplines are more detailed in the new building, whereas language and literature catalogues are more detailed in the special reading rooms of the old building. Material not represented in either the official (for staff only) or public catalogues is kept in a special catalogue, unavailable for consultation. Material such as obsolete books, pornography, foreign works unfriendly to the former Soviet Union, and works of the 'enemies of the people' (e.g., Beria, Bukharin, Radek, Trotsky) used to be confined to the limbo, or *spetsfond*, of the library but have been integrated into the main collection.

Reproduction is done by photostat only.

Russian librarians are subject specialists and know the collection in their subject field.

Useful Guides:

> Patricia K. Grimstead, *Archives and Manuscript Repositories in the U.S.S.R.: Moscow and Leningrad* (Princeton, NJ: Princeton University Press, 1972), and Supplement I Bibliographical Archives (Switzerland: Inter-Documentation, 1976)
>
> Patricia K. Grimstead, *Archives and Manuscript Repositories in the U.S.S.R.: Estonia, Latvia, Lithuania and Belorussia* (Princeton, NJ: Princeton University Press, 1981)
>
> Patricia K. Grimstead, *Archives and Manuscript Repositories in the U.S.S.R.: Ukraine and Moldavia* (Princeton, NJ; Princeton University Press, 1988). All three titles are also under the main title in microfiche.

SALTYKOV-SCHCHEDRIN STATE PUBLIC LIBRARY

SADOVAYA Ul, 18, (St Petersburg) D-69

Hours: open to all, including children of school age, from 9 A.M.– 11 P.M.

This library was formed from the Imperial Public Library and has been a depository from 1811, amassing a rich collection. Not only does it provide excellent and detailed reference service, its Bibliographics Division issues many annotated selected bibliographies annually.

NATIONAL LIBRARY OF CHINA

Beijing, 39 Baishi qiao Street, People's Republic of China (tel: 662972)
Hours: Mon.–Fri. 8 A.M. to 8 P.M.; Sun. 8 A.M. to 4 P.M.; closed Sat.

History. Founded as the Capital Library of Peking in 1910, and formally opened to the public in 1912, the National Library's collection incorporates collections formed as far back as 700 years: the Imperial Libraries of the Southern Song Dynasty (1127–1279), the Ming Dynasty (1368–1644), and other prominent collections.

Admission. There are no restrictions. Borrowing privileges are granted to individuals and institutions.

Layout. There are 15 reading rooms, some with seating capacity for 700.

Holdings. The library has 11 million volumes, including more than 5 million books (60 percent in Chinese; 40 percent in foreign languages), 4 million bound volumes of periodicals (20 percent in Chinese), 3,600 newspaper titles (50 percent in Chinese), and 580,000 volumes of rare, early printed works and rare revolutionary documents and manuscripts. The library is a depository for all publications issued in China; publishing houses must send it three copies of every title. It has exchange agreements with about 2,000 institutions in 120 countries. It collects books in the 24 national languages of the People's Republic, and English is the most frequently represented foreign language, followed by Russian, Japanese, French, German, and 109 other foreign languages.

Catalogues. Up to 1979, Chinese titles and authors are in the traditional arrangement by number of strokes and their order. Since 1979, Chinese titles and authors have been arranged in alphabetical sequence according to the Pinyin Chinese Phonetic System. The library introduced a new Chinese Classification Scheme in January 1975. (It provides 3,000 libraries in China with centralized cataloguing cards for new books in Chinese and foreign languages.)

Useful Guide:

John T. Ma, *Chinese Collections in Western Europe; Survey of their Technical and Readers' Service* (Zug. Switz.: Inter Documentation, 1985). (Notes the availability of photographic services.)

NATIONAL DIET LIBRARY (JAPAN)

1-10-1 Nagata-cho, Chiyoda-ku, Tokyo 100 (Tel: 581-2331,2341)
Hours: Mon.–Sat. 9:30 A.M.–5 P.M. (Book delivery service stops at
4 P.M.) Special Rooms: General Study Room Mon.–Fri., 9:30
A.M.–8 P.M. (for long-range study). Statutes and parliamentary
documents room, 9:30 A.M.–8 P.M. Music Library, 1 P.M.–5 P.M.
Closed Sundays, national holidays, Wednesday of the fourth week
of every month, and Dec. 28–Jan. 4.

Background. The National Diet Library inherited the collection of
the Japanese Imperial Library, which was founded as the sole
national library at the beginning of the Meiji era (1867). Since its
founding in 1948, it has acted as Japan's legal deposit library.

Admission. Admission is free but restricted to readers 20 years of
age and older. You obtain a reader's badge and reader's slips (see
Figure A.1) at the reader's gate. The slips serve as passes to the
reading room: green for the General Reading Rooms 1 and 2;
black for other reading rooms, including the Newspaper Reading
Room, the Science and Technology Materials Rooms, and the
Statutes and Parliamentary Documents Room; and red for the
General Study Room.

Layout. The first floor includes the catalogues. On the second
floor are the Central Reading Room (382 seats), General Reference Room (76 seats), Newspaper Reading Room (97 seats), UN
and Government Materials Room (12 seats), and Music Library
(14 seats). The third floor includes a second Central Reading
Room (194 seats), the General Study Room (112 seats), the Asian
and African Materials Room (32 seats), the Library Science Materials Room (32 seats), the Newspaper Clippings Room (24 seats),
Rare Book Reading Room (12 seats), Modern Political History
Materials Room (4 seats), and the Shidehara Peace Library (2
seats). On the fourth floor are the Science and Technology Materials Reading Room (59 seats), Constitutional Materials Room

Fig. A.1

National Diet Library Reader's Slip

```
Please keep this slip carefully till you leave this Library.
```

国 立 国 会 図 書 館   入   館   証

氏 名	(Name)
性 別	男 (Sex) 女	年令 (Age) 才
住 所	(Address)
職 業	(Occupation)
勤務先又は学校名	(Office or school)
ロッカー傘番号	(Locker No.)	(Umbrella No.)

日付 (Rooms)   (Seat No.)

座
席
番
号

1. 入館したらすぐ太線枠内の事項を記入して下さい。
2. この証の紛失によって事故が起った場合には、紛失した方の責任になることがありますからご注意下さい。
3. 退館の際は、この証及びバッジを閲覧者受付に返して下さい。

| 借 | (Borrowed) |
| 返 | (Returned) |

裏面に注意事項があります。

1. This reader's slip should be received at the reader's gate.
2. The number on the slip is at the same time the number of the seat assigned to the reader in the reading room.
3. When no seat number is given on the slip, the reader may go to any seat.

(17 seats), and Map Room (10 seats). The fifth floor holds the Statutes and Parliamentary Documents Room (44 seats).

There is a photocopying service.

Requesting Books. Because it is basically a closed-stack library, you must file call slips at the central circulation counter (see Figure A.2). As a foreigner, you should write your name in block letters, or preferably in *katakana*. When the books or journals arrive from the stacks, you will be paged. Show your reader's slip and have the 'borrowed' column rubber-stamped. When finished, you return the materials to the counter that received them from the stacks

Fig. A.2

National Diet Library Call Slip

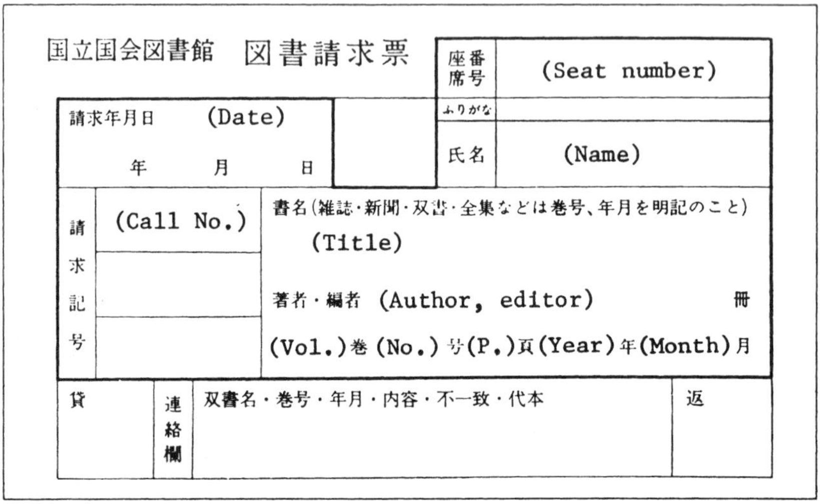

国立国会図書館　図書請求票	座番 席号	(Seat number)	
請求年月日　　(Date) 　　年　　　月　　　日	ふりがな 氏名	(Name)	
請 求 記 号	(Call No.)	書名(雑誌・新聞・双書・全集などは巻号、年月を明記のこと) 　(Title) 著者・編者　(Author, editor)　　　　　冊 (Vol.)巻 (No.)号(P.)頁(Year)年(Month)月
貸	連 絡 欄	双書名・巻号・年月・内容・不一致・代本	返

and have the 'returned' column of your reader's slip rubber-stamped. Your badges and slips are returned to the officer at the readers' gate. You cannot take books out of the library.

U.S. LIBRARY OF CONGRESS

101 Independence Avenue, Washington DC, 20540 (Tel: 202-707-5000)
Hours: General Reading Rooms: 8:30 A.M.–9:30 P.M., Mon., Wed., Thurs.; 8:30 A.M.–5 P.M. on Tues., Fri., Sat.

The largest library in the United States, the Library of Congress serves primarily congresspersons but is open to the general public over high-school age. No reading ticket is required. The library operates like the New York Public Library. Readers fill out request slips for books and periodicals.

Reading Rooms. There are two general reading rooms: the Main Reading Room on the first floor of the Thomas Jefferson Building, and the Thomas Jefferson Reading Room on the fifth floor of the John Adams Building (nearby, between Second and Third Streets, S.E.). Books from the general collections may be requested in either of these rooms, but you should use the reading room in the building that houses the collections you want to consult. There are 20 specialized reading rooms, many of them covering the subjects of the special divisions of the New York Public Library.

Unlike the New York Public Library, however, the Library of Congress has a Law Library; this is one of the most comprehensive collections of legal materials ever developed, in all languages and covering all legal systems, both ancient and modern. You can find reference assistance and access to relevant Law Library collections through the Anglo-American Reading Room on the second floor of the Jefferson Building and in international and foreign law through the European, Far Eastern, Hispanic, and Near Eastern and African Law Divisions. There is a National Library Service for the Blind and Handicapped at 1291 Taylor Street, N.W.

In addition are the U.S. Copyright Office and the Congressional Research Service.

The Copyright Office of the Library of Congress (James Madison Memorial Building, 101 Independence Avenue, S.E., Washington, DC, 20559) is open to the public from 8:30 A.M. to 5 P.M. Monday through Friday (except for legal holidays). The various records freely available to the public include an extensive card catalogue, an automated catalogue containing records from 1978 forward, record books, and microfilm records of assignments and related documents. Other records, including correspondence file and deposit copies, are not open to the public for searching. They may be inspected, however, on request and a payment of a $10-per-hour search fee.

The Congressional Research Service does searches only for members of Congress (about a half-million searches a year). Its Selective Dissemination of Information service provides congressional patrons with photocopies of the text of citations available in an online database. It uses microcomputer and telecommunications technology in its internal operations. The public's access is limited to reading *CRS Review*, which features current topics of major legislative interest in magazine format, and *CRS Studies in the Public Domain*, a semiannual listing of all the CRS research products that have been printed by the Congress and are available as committee prints, House or Senate documents or reports, or insertions in the Congressional Record.

Catalogues. The Main Catalog (beginning in the Main Reading Room and extending into the adjoining rooms and corridor) contains printed author, title, and subject cards interfiled into a single alphabetical sequence. (In the Thomas Jefferson Reading Room you have to use printed book catalogues adjacent to the reading room.) At the end of the card catalogue is the Computer Catalog Center, which provides online information on English-language books catalogued from 1968 to the present and on books in most other Western languages added since 1973. The catalogues in the special reading rooms, especially those of the Rare Book and Special Collections Reading Room, also supplement the general catalogues.

A separate catalogue of serials adjoins the Main Catalog, and a list of the most frequently used periodicals, with call numbers included, is available at the Central and the Reference desks. There is also a serials catalogue in the Science Reading Room, adjacent to the Thomas Jefferson Reading Room. Before visiting the Library of Congress, you can check its holdings in its printed book catalogues or in the NUC (see p. 81) found in other research libraries. Its online catalogue is Locis, with over 30 million records, and is available over the Internet. See the Library's homepage (http://www.loc.gov/). The Library of Congress Internet site under 'Searching Other Catalogs' provides Internet links to the catalogues of research and university institutions around the world.

The Library's SCORPIO computer system gives you access to cataloguing and other information in four separate databases:

(1) the Computerized Catalogue for books accessioned after 1968; (2) the Bibliographic Citation File, for periodical articles and government publications on public policy subjects for the current year and the two previous years; (3) the Legislative Files, for public bills and resolutions introduced into Congress for the current and the two previous Congresses; and (4) the National Referral Center File, for information on selected research organizations that answer inquiries from the public.

You are instructed on the use of the computer in the Computer Catalog Center.

Digital Optical Disc and Analog Videodisk Technology. Using special terminals located in some of the reading rooms, you can identify articles whose text has been put on disc, view them on the terminal screen, and print them out immediately. Analog videodisk technology permits storage of up to 108,000 low-resolution colour or black-and-white images on the two sides of a disk. It serves to preserve from decay not only print but also nonprint materials (e.g., prints, photographs, motion pictures), to reduce retrieval time, to provide unlimited storage capacity, and to eliminate the 'not-on-shelf' and 'missing' reports common to all libraries.

THE LIBRARY OF PARLIAMENT (CANADA)

Parliament Hill, Ottawa, Canada, K1A 0A9
Hours: Fluctuate. Tel: 613-995-1166. Internet site: http://www.parl.gc.ca

With the democratizing of governments in the 1990s, parliamentary libraries are being established in many countries. The Parliamentary Services Section of the International Federation of Library Associations and Institutions (IFLA) (http://www.ifla.org) has published *World Directory of National Parliamentary Libraries, World Directory of Parliamentary Libraries of Federated States and Autonomous Territories, Parliamentary Libraries of Latin America,* and *Parliamentary Libraries of Central and Eastern Europe and the Former*

Soviet Union. Although these libraries primarily serve the legislators and press corps with background and current information on government business and the social and economic ramifications of government programs, they can provide individual researchers with information that cannot be found elsewhere. For instance, the Canadian Parliamentary Library provides information on government and the library's role to the public on the one hand, but does studies and analyses for parliamentarians and others that are not made available to the public on the other hand. Its online system (PARLCAT) can be accessed only within the library. The public can obtain information on Parliament from the library by calling (613) 992–4793.

Admission: The library is restricted to the governor general, members of the Privy Council, members of the Senate and the House of Commons, officers of the two Houses, Justices of the Supreme Court of Canada and of the Exchequer Court, members of the Press Gallery, and academic researchers; the latter must receive written consent from either the Speaker of the House or the Senate or the Parliamentary Librarian.

Organization: The Library has three branches of operation: (1) the Information and Documentation Branch, (2) the Parliamentary Research Branch, and (3) the Administrative and Personnel Branch.

The Information and Documentation Branch consists of four divisions: (a) the Public Service Division provides information for patrons and teaches users how to use the library effectively; (b) the Collections Division purchases and preserves the collection and keeps parliamentarians up-to-date with current events; (c) the Cataloguing and Indexing Division is responsible for indexing and subject analysis services; (d) the Systems Divison deals with automation and computer services. This branch prepares bibliographies and compilations, and maintains a clipping service from 20 daily papers from across the nation.

The Parliamentary Research Branch has four divisions: the Economics Division, the Science and Technology Division, the

Political and Social Affairs Division, and the Law and Government Division. They offer a research and consulting service for parliamentarians, an outreach program to aid the branches and agencies of the federal government, and an assistance service for committees. This branch publishes four types of publications for general distribution to parliamentarians: *Current Issue Reviews* (concise, descriptive commentaries on topical issues), *Legislative Summaries* (brief analyses prepared for most government bills), *Backgrounds* (in-depth studies), and *Mini-Reviews* (brief papers on newsworthy events).

The Administrative and Personnel Branch comprises the Executive Office, Management and Administration and Support Services divisions, which do the accounting, hiring, training, records management, and payment of staff.

The Collection: With more than 600,000 items, it covers a wide range of subjects, including Canadian political and parliamentary affairs, law, parliamentary history and procedure, political science, international relations, sociology, and historical documents dating back to the nation's beginnings. It maintains a rare-book collection, a foreign parliamentary publications collection, and a collection of manuscripts on Canadian politics and politicians. These collections are found at six locations on Parliament Hill and are accessed through a network of computer terminals. This network is linked to other federal government libraries, including the National Library of Canada, which, along with the neighbouring National Archives, offers free access near Parliament Hill to researchers. Altogether they provide a rich resource. The library provides an interlibrary loan service 'of last resort.' It also has a rich oral-history collection of parliamentarians from the 1970s and 1980s.

Catalogues and Layout: The Parliamentary Library consists of the main library with a reading room and closed stacks in the Parliament Buildings and three branch libraries: the branch library in the Confederation Building is specifically dedicated to general information whereas the branch library in the Wellington Building is oriented to political studies and data. The online catalogue, PARLCAT, locates books, serials, articles, audio-visual materials, and most government documents held by the library. PARLCD is the library's CD-ROM network of bibliographic and full-text data-bases and may be searched from parliamentarians' offices on the Hill.

Access to Government Information. Freedom-of-information laws have been passed at all levels of government. You will have to find the procedures to be used to obtain the information. There are manuals of procedures published for finding your way through the maze of departments and requirements for some govern-ments, but for many you will have to make inquiries of govern-ment offices on how to proceed or perhaps get help from a major newspaper that routinely files requests for covert government information. Such a service at the national level may be and should be provided to the public by parliamentary libraries.

Brief Bibliography

Most guides to libraries and research use the bibliographic approach; some deal with special fields, such as John E. Pemberton, *British Official Publications* (Oxford: Pergamon, 1973), and Judith S. Robinson, *Subject Guide to U.S. Government Reference Sources* (Littleton, CO: Libraries Unlimited, 1985). Others list books under subject of research, such as David Bryant, *Finding Information the Library Way: A Guide to Reference Sources* (Hamden, CT: Library Professional Publishers, 1987), and Grant W. Morse, *Concise Guide to Library Research* (New York: Fleet Academic, 1975), or by specific subject department, such as the following:

Law:
Morris Cohen and Robert Behring, *How to Find the Law* (St Paul: West, 1983), or Margaret Banks, *Using a Law Library,* 4th ed. (Toronto: Carswell, 1985).

Medicine:
Leslie Morton, *How to Use a Medical Library,* 4th ed. (London: Heinemann, 1964).

Genealogy:
Gilbert Doane, *Searching for Your Ancestors* (Minneapolis: University of Minnesota, 1980).
Noel Stevenson, *Search and Research: The Researcher's Handbook: A Guide to Official Records and Library Sources for Investigators, Historians, Genealogists, Lawyers and Librarians* (Salt Lake City: Desert Book, 1973).

General guides like Robert Balay's *Guide to Reference Books,* 11th ed. (Chicago: ALA, 1996) will provide a list of the major reference works in most fields. Rather than provide a lengthy bibliography of the publications referred to in this book, I include a brief list of reference books of immediate usefulness by subject department to give you an idea of the kind of book you can expect the department to have.

SCIENCE AND TECHNOLOGY

Computer Abstracts, 1956

Dictionary of Inorganic Compounds (New York: Chapman and Hall, 1992). Also on CD-ROM and online at HEILBRON.

Dictionary of Organic Compounds, 5th ed. and Supplement (New York: Chapman and Hall, 1982). Also on CD-ROM and the online database HEILBRON.

Dictionary of Organometallic Compounds, annual supplements (New York: Chapman and Hall, 1984). Also online at HEILBRON.

Encyclopedia of Chemical Processing and Design (New York: Marcel Decker, 1976–).

Kirk-Othmer Encyclopedia of Chemical Technology, 3rd ed., vols. 1–24, Index, and Supplements (New York: Wiley, 1984). Also available on CD-ROM and online.

Mitchell Manuals for Automotive Professionals (San Diego: Mitchell, 1981).

Sweets Catalog: Products for Industrial Construction and Renovation, 4 vols., annual (a collection of manufacturers' catalogues).

ECONOMICS

Dictionary of Occupational Titles (Washington, DC: U.S. Labor Department, 1991).

Editor and Publisher. Market Guide, annual (New York: 1924–).

(Munn's) *Encyclopedia of Banking and Finance* (Chicago: Probus, 1993).

Encyclopedia of Business Information Sources (Detroit: Gale, 1970–)

Index of Economic Articles in Journals and Collective Volumes, annual (Homewood, IL: R.D. Irwin, 1884/1924–). Also on CD-ROM as *EconLit* and online as *Economic Literature Index.*

Standard Directory of Advertisers, annual (New York: National Register Publishing, 1964–). Also on CD-ROM.

Standard & Poor's Register of Corporations, Directors and Executives, annual (New York: Standard & Poor's Corp., 1928–). Also on CD-ROM and online in COMPUSTAT.

Standard Rate and Data Service (Skokie, IL: 1919–) (a series of separate publications published irregularly).

Thomas' Register of American Manufacturers and Thomas' Register Catalog File, annual (New York: Thomas Publishing Co., 1909–) Also on CD-ROM and online, updated semiannually.

HUMANITIES

Access: The Supplementary Index to Periodicals (Syracuse, NY: 1975–). Also on CD-ROM and online.

Bibliography of American Literature, by J.N. Blanck (New Haven: Yale University Press, 1955–91).

Cambridge Bibliography of English Literature (Cambridge: Cambridge University Press, 1940–77).

Canada Year Book, annual (Ottawa: Statistics Canada, 1906–).

Celebrity Register (New York: International Inc., 1986).

Cole's Cross Reference Directory, annual (New York).

The Dictionary of Art, 34 vols (New York: Grove's Dictionaries, 1996).

Encyclopedia of Black America (New York: McGraw-Hill, 1981).

(Bartlett's) *Familiar Quotations* (Boston: Little, Brown, 1992).

Granger's Index to Poetry (New York: Columbia University Press, 1994). Also on CD-ROM as *Columbia Granger's World of Poetry.*

Guinness Book of Sports Records, annual (New York: Facts on File, 1991–).

Handbook of Latin American Studies, 2 vols, annual (Austin: University of Texas, 1936–).

Harvard Guide to American History (Cambridge: Belknap Press, 1974).

Holidays and Anniversaries of the World (Detroit: Gale, 1985).

Hotel and Motel Red Book, annual (New York: American Hotel Association, 1886–1990); continued by *OAG Business Travel Planner,* quarterly (1990–).

Literary Market Place, annual (New York: Bowker, 1940–).

MLA Handbook for Writers of Research Papers, 2nd ed., by Joseph Gibaldi and Walter S. Achtert (New York: Modern Language Association, 1984) ('a set of conventions governing the written presentation of research').

MLA International Bibliography of Books and Articles on the Modern Languages and Literatures, annual (New York: Modern Language Association, 1921–). Also on CD-ROM and online through OCLC *FirstSearch.*

Martindale-Hubbell Law Directory, annual (New York: Martindale-Hubbell, 1931–).

National Union Catalog, pre-1956 imprints, 685 vols (London: Mansell, 1968–80).

Psychological Abstracts, monthly (Lancaster, PA: 1927–). Also on CD-ROM as *PsycLIT* and online.

The Reader's Adviser: A Layman's Guide to Literature, 6 vols (New York: Bowker, 1986–88).

Scott's Standard Postage Stamp Catalog, annual (New York: Scott Publishing, 1867–).

A Short-Title Catalogue of Books Printed in England, Scotland and Ireland, Wales, and British America. 1641–1700, 3 vols (New York: Columbia University Press, 1945–51).

Who's Who in America, A Biographical Dictionary of Notable Living Men and Women, biennial (Chicago: Marquis, 1899–).

Working Press of the Nation, annual in 5 vols (New York: Farrell Publishing, 1945–) (a catalogue of newspaper, magazine, TV and radio, feature writing, photographer, internal publications).

World of Learning, annual (London: Allen & Unwin, 1947–).

Index